# Strategic Requirements Analysis

*Karl Cox is the world's foremost expert on strategic requirements. He's helped countless businesses achieve success where other analysts have failed. If you reside at the pointy tip where business strategy and technology meet, this book is a must-read. For those who wish to be at the top of their game and masters of their domain, this book shows you how.*

Steven Bleistein, CEO, Relansa, Inc., Japan

*What I love about this book is the thorough coverage of probably the most important part of the requirements process, the art of gaining knowledge from the client. Even better, is the clear and accessible style, guiding the reader through by reference to real cases. I would recommend this book to any student of software requirements, and will definitely recommend it to my own students.*

Keith Phalp, Bournemouth University, UK

# Strategic Requirements Analysis

*From Interviews to Models*

KARL A. COX
*University of Brighton, Sussex, UK*

Routledge
Taylor & Francis Group

LONDON AND NEW YORK

First published 2015 by Gower Publishing

2 Park Square, Milton Park, Abingdon, Oxfordshire OX14 4RN
52 Vanderbilt Avenue, New York, NY 10017

*Routledge is an imprint of the Taylor & Francis Group, an informa business*

First issued in paperback 2020

**British Library Cataloguing in Publication Data**
A catalogue record for this book is available from the British Library.

**Library of Congress Cataloging-in-Publication Data**
Cox, Karl A.
   Strategic requirements analysis : from interviews to models / by Karl A. Cox.
       pages cm
   Includes bibliographical references and index.
   ISBN 978-1-4724-7472-8 (hardback : alk. paper) – ISBN 978-1-4724-7473-5 (ebook) – ISBN 978-1-4724-7474-2 (epub)
   1. Employment interviewing. I. Title.

   HF5549.5.I6C69 2015
   658.3'1124–dc23
                                                                                    2015024537


ISBN 13: 978-1-4724-7472-8 (hbk)
ISBN 13: 978-0-367-60606-0 (pbk)

# Contents

# List of Figures

# List of Tables

# Preface

## What are Strategic Requirements?

A strategic requirement is something an organisation sets out to achieve to help it in its business endeavours. The term 'strategic requirement' as used in this book is generic. A strategic requirement could be the long-term Vision the organisation sets itself. A strategic requirement could be the key business requirement that needs to be achieved for a specific project to be deemed a success. A strategic requirement could be a business goal or a business strategy to achieve that goal. A set of strategic requirements defines the structure of goals, strategies and tactics that organisations need to put in place in order to give them direction and impetus in any business undertaking. A strategic requirement is not a business process but a business process helps achieve strategic requirements. A strategic requirement is not the same as an IT requirement but an IT requirement could be of strategic intent.

Business analysts and consultants need to understand strategic requirements in order to understand where projects, whether technical or not, are going to deliver benefits to business and where they are not. The ability to be able to gather, analyse, model and present strategic requirements is key to the role of business analysts and consultants. Without this ability and understanding, a business analyst will not be able to take that forward step to becoming an enterprise analyst.

## Interviews

If you're reading this, you've been interviewed before. If you've ever had a job, you most likely had to get through an interview or several to assess if you're the right person for the post. If you've been to the doctor, you would have been interviewed to find out what was wrong with you. We've all had that experience before. But what if you were the interviewer? What would you do if you had to interview someone or several people? We've all been in interviews where the interviewer didn't appear to know what he or she wanted. Occasionally, you may even have been interviewed by someone who appeared to be very well organised, who asked searching questions, who made you feel relaxed and got you answering questions without realising it. These interviewers are rarer than you think. Most interviews are very unsatisfactory for both parties. As an interviewee you may have come out of the interview wondering what happened, why you weren't given an opportunity to put your case or make your point as you had expected or had been told, why you were asked seemingly random, unrelated questions. Why had the interview taken an hour longer than you were told it would, making you late for your next appointment? To make matters worse, the interviewer ran out of ink when taking notes and had to borrow your pen. Or didn't take any notes at all, so how was he supposed to remember anything important you said?

This interviewer hadn't planned things too well. But just what should an interviewer plan for? Surely interviews are just conversations with people? Actually, interviews are not at all mere conversations, though the best interviewers make it appear so. What good interviewers are best at is finding out the right information in a calm, polite, well-organised and timely manner.

But when you come to running an interview for the first time, it's hard to get it right. If you're a seasoned campaigner, it's always good to sharpen your techniques from time to time to keep getting the most out of interviews, otherwise you slacken off and you miss things that you know you shouldn't have. This book is a guide for people who have to conduct interviews. It describes a process, guidelines and ideas for conducting interviews – all of which have been tried and tested successfully in practice by me and by others I have worked with.

## Models

Models are really useful as a way to organise, analyse and present information that has been captured in the interview process. If you've gone to the trouble to interview a number of people about their strategic requirements, it is a sensible idea to do some analysis. Why? Because you'll find that one view is only a blinkered view of the world and there are lot of people with blinkers on. So you have to decipher what people say in order to come to a consensus of some kind – most people think this, or that and so on, even if it does go against what the official policy is.

There are lots of ways to represent information: text is the most common, then there are tables and then there are models. So why model if modelling is last in line? Well, text is often hard to read – pulling the key information from all those hundreds of thousands of words is often too hard. Tables are good in that you can structure text systematically so that key information is well represented. We use tables in this book to do just that. But tables don't go far enough. A model will show you how words can be visualised and placed on a page, showing order of importance, showing direction, cause and effect explicitly, showing ownership. These are key concepts that are very hard to convey when just using words or indeed tables. The saying 'a picture paints a thousand words' could not be more true.

## Is This Book for Me?

If you need to conduct interviews then this book is for you. If you're looking for scientific theory or psychology, you won't find it here. If you're looking for that journalistic headline question, that's not here either but if you're a business-IT consultant/contractor/analyst or a student about to embark on a project/assignment along the lines of discovering and modelling business or technical requirements, then this book is good for you. If you want to take the findings from your interviews and turn them into meaningful models to show your clients/customers/team/supervisors, then this a good book for you. It could help you even if you've had 20 years working in this sector. There may be nuggets you hadn't thought about before. Hopefully it is straightforward, too.

## Do We Really Need Another Book on Business Analysis?

I come from a world of business–IT consulting and research, particularly into how to find out about business strategies, business processes and IT requirements. Though there are a multitude of texts in these areas, all of them are concerned with modelling and almost none of them have much to say about elicitation/gathering requirements – getting the information from your customer in the first place. There are a few good books on getting IT requirements: Ian Alexander and Ljerka Beus-Dukic have written an excellent book on this.[1] And they have a short introduction on conducting interviews. But given that elicitation forms such a big part of requirements management, it is surprising how little is written about it or taught on university programmes – many academics and researchers seem to confuse elicitation and modelling.

---

1   Ian Alexander and Ljerka Beus-Dukic, *Discovering Requirements: How to Specify Products and Services*, Chichester, Wiley 2009.

These are not the same thing at all. In a recent and damning report on the state of business analysis practice, IAG Consulting surveyed over 100 medium to large companies about the state of their *strategic* IT projects (budgeted on average at US$3 million) and found that 68 per cent are failing because their business analysis and requirements skills were not adequate; a significant factor was poor requirements discovery practices.[2] One of the many important skills a business analyst needs in requirements discovery is the ability to effectively plan, conduct and manage a set of interviews to get the requirements right, be they strategic, operational or IT-oriented. This book sets out to provide some of those skills but from a strategic perspective.

There is a lot about modelling here too and the reason for that is to connect the dots. When all is said and done and you've got data from a lot of interviews (and other sources, not addressed here), how do you turn that mass of data into a meaningful business strategy model that can bring light to the oblique world of business–IT analysis? There are a lot of books on modelling but not much that I've seen on this kind of modelling. There are a lot of books and academic articles on goal modelling in the 'requirements engineering' literature but there isn't much that's effectively in-depth end-to-end. There is only so much that one can cover in a paper because of its word limit so a book is an opportunity to go into more depth.

## Why I Wrote This Book

The idea for the book arose for a number of reasons. One reason why was a conversation I once had with a former colleague a number of years ago. He called me into his office and looked somewhat flustered. Our conversation went like this:

| | |
|---|---|
| *Me:* | *What's up?* |
| *Colleague:* | *Have you ever interviewed people before?* |
| *Me:* | *Yes, lots of them.* |
| *Colleague:* | *What, real people?* |
| *Me:* | *Yes, is there any other kind?* |
| *Colleague:* | *I'm never doing it again, I just interviewed five people.* |
| *Me:* | *That's great, so what happened?* |

---

2   Keith Ellis, *Business Analysis Benchmark: The Impact of Business Requirements on the Success of Technology Projects*, IAG Consulting 2009.

*Colleague: They didn't give me the answers I wanted to hear. I'm*
*never interviewing anyone again ...*

Having conducted countless interviews in nearly 15 years of consulting and research work, I have come to realise that interviewing is more than having a chat or talking off the top of your head or not getting the answers you wanted to hear. Along the way, I've learned that planning before you go into the interview on what questions you're going to ask is a good idea, and then actually asking those questions is even better. Writing down the answers helped some, too! Being flexible also mattered. If an interviewee told me some nuggets I hadn't thought to ask about at all, I would listen and make notes – I learned not to be blinkered in sticking to my questions. I'd then ask some other people about those nuggets to cross check them. And at the other end of the interview, I came to realise that presenting feedback for validation could either enrage or delight the interviewee – depending on how you present it.

The primary tool consultants and business analysts use for communication is talking. Although email and text/instant messaging might be eating into that usage, and there are lots of different techniques to get information, ultimately as a business analyst or consultant or even a researcher you still will spend the majority of your time talking with people.

If you can't present all that incredible information back to your client effectively in one page, then it is hard for them and you to get to grips rapidly with what is going on. So being able to present a model is really useful because it provides structure and a visual format to aid understanding, discussion and next steps. So it is worth the effort to join the dots, which this book is all about.

## Limitations

This book isn't about the theory of strategy or interviews – it is a practical book. This book isn't all you need to know as an analyst or modeller; there are many other approaches out there that can assist you also. This book isn't about specification, so there's scant mention of it here. There are many excellent resources on that. The book is about taking an interview and modelling the results. Useful, for sure. All you're ever need? Unlikely.

# Acknowledgements

Thank you to my students and colleagues at the University of Brighton who have been part of this book. Thank you to all the companies I have worked with so I could put these ideas into practice. Thank you especially to Dr Steven Bleistein and Professor June Verner who I worked with in Australia and Japan. Steve came up with much of the idea of goal modelling and connecting context in his PhD from other research and his practical experiences in business. What you will read from here on is a simplification and extension of that academic and practical research – all faults found here on in are entirely my own.

# Introduction

## Why Do Interviews?

If you don't ask, you won't get, simply put. Questions are never indiscrete if asked in 'ignorance' or 'innocence'. You do interviews to find out answers to difficult, challenging and sometimes career or life-changing issues or opportunities. In terms of gathering information, Chapters 1–4 are only about interviews because almost no one teaches interviewing skills these days; I regularly get told that there's no point teaching interviewing because it's 'so easy and just obvious'. Yet if conducting an interview appears to be so easy to get right then why does it so often feel unfulfilling? This book will give you useful insights into preparing, conducting, analysing and presenting feedback from interviews. But why do interviews if there are other approaches out there,[1] especially if interviews don't go well so often? A key point of conducting interviews is you gather masses of really useful information that is often otherwise inaccessible. The amount of information can be overwhelming but there are ways to analyse it effectively. You can create models of what people say about their activities, about what organisations really need. Interviews allow you to surreptitiously[2] cross reference information from different sources. For instance, if you've had conflicting opinions about the functionality of a certain IT system, you might want to check with different users that the system has the needed functionality or works effectively for each user group. *Do* say something like: 'There appear to be a number of issues with the finance reporting system. Do you have any experience with it? What do you do with it? What are the issues you've found? How would you fix them?' If you're smart enough to say this, you'll get great responses such as:

- 'I hate that system – it doesn't allow me to input the right data.'

- 'I can never get the data I need out of it.'

---

1   There are many ways to gather information from people, and these are well documented. Don't assume interviewing is the only technique out there – you should always try to triangulate what you learn from interviews with learnings from other techniques.

2   I use the word 'surreptitiously' because it is not a good idea to openly contradict someone in an interview, nor to say something like: 'Oh, Norman said it was because of this.' Don't name names, ever. It pays to be more subtle.

- 'There's nothing wrong with it at all and I use it every day.'

- 'I don't use that system, you need to talk to Bill – from what he says, it sucks. But you'd better ask him as he's responsible for putting in the monthly reports.'

The purpose of analysis is that we want to find out something. What's the best way to do this? Ask. Couldn't an email suffice? Well, no. Actually, there's more to an interview than just the spoken words. Much more information can be elicited from an interview than a simple verbatim transcription of what was said. Like what? Emotion. You get to see the emotion.

One of the biggest benefits from conducting interviews is you can see which of the interviewee's buttons you've pressed that causes a powerful emotional response. But don't deliberately attempt to upset your interviewee as that path will lead you quickly to the end of the interview and the end of your engagement. An online survey won't tell you what really mattered to the interviewee, what made her grimace, what made him turn away or blink or rub an ear lobe or scratch his nose. You have to be there to see it. These emotional responses are also the perfect indicators to you for how you conduct yourself, for what you ask next and how you ask it. Are you scaring your interviewees? Do they all act like mice? Or do they walk all over you and confidently sound off whatever is on their mind? The way your interviewee acts and responds tells you a lot about how good a job you are doing. You should be having an exchange of equals.

There are other reasons to interview. Reading the user manual doesn't tell you anything about what features on an accounting system the payroll team avoids. You only find out these things when you ask.

A cautionary note: you're not the agony aunt. You're not meant to be a shoulder to cry on. But you can be. If this is the only way you get a response out of an interviewee, then so be it. But remember that heat of the moment, emotion-laden responses are not always well thought through, nor are they always the most sensible suggestions.

## If Interviewing is So Great, Why Do I Need to Do Other Research?

There's a downside to interviewing. Though this book discusses interviewing at length as a way of gathering information, don't assume this is all you will ever need to do. Interviewing on its own is not always enough to give you the full picture. Saying that, of course, interviews will get you a long way there if you do them right. However, for the record here are some of the pitfalls/risks of *only* interviewing:

- Triangulation of disparate viewpoints[3] is difficult – if you don't have any other viewpoints. This means you cannot easily cross reference responses to other sources of information and data.

- Information overload: you may get so much information that you won't have time to analyse it and too much information will get in the way of what you really need to find out.

- The wrong people tell you the wrong things but they do sound credible – deciphering the credible from the incredible is hard.

- Interviewing large numbers of stakeholders is time-consuming and exhausting.

- Interviewees have tunnel vision – you only ever get one perspective.

- Presenting an argument is fraught with risk as it is one sided. As a case in point look at the following scenario.

## SCENARIO: DIFFERENT APPROACHES TO INFORMATION GATHERING YIELDS DIFFERENT RESULTS

I once conducted a series of interviews to find out a business process for a media equipment rental outfit that wanted to add more IT support to their process. So I interviewed all staff who rented out equipment and formed a model of the process. I then got the staff to simulate what they normally did in a role play. Guess what? Different process. Then I observed the staff in their daily jobs. Guess what? Different process again. It turns out that neither the role play nor the real work was quite right according to their management. What I'd been told in the interviews was the official process but the reality was different. So when faced between the choice of theory or reality, you should always err on the side of reality.

If there are so many downsides to interviewing, why bother doing it? Surely other techniques will be better, cheaper, faster, I hear you ask.

---

3    Information gathered by other means such as workshops, reading documents and observation.

Well, there's an upside to interviewing, or did I forget to mention that? Interviews get you talking with *real* people. That's it? Only one benefit? Yes! This reason alone far outweighs all the downsides combined because you can ask what you want. You might not get a sensible answer but you can follow a train of thought that only a real person would have implanted in your head. Only a real person can point you in the direction of another real person you really have to talk to, even though they are not on your list. Finally, by talking to experts – the real people – you will, by proxy, tread the path to becoming a de facto expert. You pick up the language interviewees use, you learn the context they work in. You can begin to have a meaningful conversation with your customer.

## This is about Real People

Remember you are dealing with real people. This is an important fact. You need a decorum becoming of the circumstances: you have been paid to talk to a lot of people and find out things, those people have been volunteered by their management or peers or have chosen to talk with you, if asked, or might throw themselves at you in a bid to get their oar in. Here are some key criteria for conducting interviews that will keep your focus on the fact that these are real people:

- Tell the truth – your integrity is far more important than the next pay cheque; in fact, your integrity is priceless. If you are asked to misrepresent your client, yourself, the facts as you know them or to mask the real reason for the interview, think seriously about working for someone else. You know this anyway, but it is easy to get caught up in the excitement.

- Be independent – conduct interviews with your team and only your team. There are situations where you will be pressured to work in tandem with one of your client's team in an interview or series of interviews. Don't do it. If you are to be considered a credible and reliable consultant or interviewer or researcher, do the work yourself and very politely refuse to work with your client. The reason why you were hired as an external consultant/researcher is because you are external – and damned good at your job. (Of course, if you're employed in the same company as your interviewees then ignore this point.) Convincing your client that you work better alone should not be an issue – the client should expect you to work independently. That's why you were hired. See the scenario below.

- Avoid the boss! By all means, interview your client if he/she is involved. Just don't do it with other employees in the room and expect to interview them at the same time. They will only ever agree with the boss or will clam up. This isn't always the case, you do get the occasional exception where an employee will take a calculated risk and criticise or make bold/brash statements about restructuring the company in front of the boss.

## SCENARIO: STAFF ARE UNPREPARED TO TALK IN FRONT OF THEIR BOSS

A colleague of mine was hired to investigate risk management practices in an organisation after a serious of publicised IT project fiascos. Part of my colleague's remit was to interview a number of staff about their experiences on projects and how risks had been dealt with. Because the organisation was so concerned that its employees would paint its practices in a bad light, the organisation insisted on having a senior member of staff present at all interviews in case the interviewee blurted out anything deemed risky to the reputation of the organisation. The net result of this tactic was that, of the 16 or so interviews conducted, none of the interviewees said much at all beyond their name, role and some bland statements about how the organisation was successful. The engagement ended in near failure because no interviewee was willing to comment on anything risky. My colleague told me the whole post mortem review engagement was a political sham.

Whatever the situation you find yourself in, remember you are talking with real people and you will have an impact on their lives. It is an important responsibility and one you need to handle professionally. Make sure you give justice to yourself by being well prepared in order to give an opportunity to your interviewee.

## Time is Not on Your Side

Interviews can be time consuming. Conducting an interview involves a great deal more than just sitting down for an hour for a chat. So how long do you think it takes to do interviews, perform analysis, write up and present findings? This is one of those 'how-long-is-a-piece-of-string' questions. A general rule of thumb is it is going to take a whole lot longer than you thought or planned for! I've listed in the Table I.1 how long it normally takes me to go through the end-to-end process. Once you get up to speed, you can use the ideas presented in this book on a regular basis and establish criteria for determining what you do and don't do from the list. When you reach this stage then please add in your own numbers and see what you get. The table assumes you have 20 interviews to do.

**Table I.1     Interview time frame for 20 interviews**

| Activity | Hours per Interview | Total Hours | Accumulated Hours |
|---|---|---|---|
| Conduct interview | 1 | 20 | 20 |
| Transcribe interview | 1 | 20 | 40 |
| Conduct analysis | 1 | 20 | 60 |
| Triangulate analysis results | 0.5 | 10 | 70 |
| Write one-pager/interim report | 0.5 | 10 | 80 |
| Validation feedback | 0.5 | 10 | 90 |
| Rework | 0.5 | 10 | 100 |
| Presentation layout | 0.5 | 10 | 120 |
| Model creation | 1 | 20 | 140 |
| Final report write up | 2 | 40 | **160 hours** |

As you can see from the last row of Table I.1, the whole interview process can take up to 160 hours – that is, four weeks full time for one person working 40 hours per week. And that is twice as long as your customer is willing to give you!

And the list doesn't include things like:

- time taken to arrange the interviews;

- time taken to plan and prepare the interviews, including practice runs if needed;

- time taken to read up on background context and official documents prior to and in between interviews;

- time taken to present feedback;

- time taken in travelling to and from interview locations.

So what are the implications of this?

Table I.1 assumes you use all appropriate planning, interviewing, analysis, modelling and documenting techniques, as presented in this book. You may decide that some are not necessary, nor appropriate. Validation feedback assumes you spend up to another 30 minutes with each interviewee to get feedback on findings and ask further questions. As you read through this book, you'll see that I seriously do not recommend you do this with all interviewees. However, there are circumstances where you might, hence its inclusion in Table I.1. You may have to make the decision not to analyse some interviews because you don't have enough time and might well decide to analyse only the most interesting or most important interviewees or only some of the questions asked. I've allowed one full week to write the final report. This may seem excessive but you may need more time, especially if your findings need to fit into a wider strategic analysis, business case, requirements document or review document, and you also need to present slides. You will have to go through several revisions and edits before you submit your report.

If you do have only three weeks to conduct and report back on the interviews, you will need to get help, either in conducting the analysis, in report writing or in conducting interviews in parallel with you so that double the 'normal' amount of interviews and analysis can be done in one day. This will alter how you charge if you are a consultant. This last point may or may not affect your thinking about time frames. If you are a lone business analyst (BA) for hire, an independent consultant or working in a boutique consulting business, you'll already know that government agencies have budget ceilings for hiring consultants on projects. It works like this: national-level agencies may have a ceiling of, say, £20,000 for 'discretionary' hire of consultants. If you put in a proforma that is costed at more than £20,000 or the agency states it requires bids within a certain price range above the £20,000, then the agency is obliged to put out a general call for tender. You can't afford to wait that long and suddenly you've got a lot of competitors beating at your prospect's door. County or regional-level agencies may have an even lower ceiling of, for example, £10,000[4] before they have to put out a call for tender. You'll need to weigh up the engagement's prospective scope of work against the sensible maximum pay you can ask for – just below the ceiling – to avoid it going to tender. What you decide to take on may cost you more than the monetary value of the engagement. Think about it: it will normally take a month or two to get the engagement underway from its initial light bulb idea in your client's head. You'll spend one to two months doing the work and then wait one to

---

4   Note these figures are examples only in order to explain a common situation in many
    countries.

two months to get paid. All in, that could be six months to earn £10,000 before tax, before paying bills such as staff salaries, operational costs and overheads. What's left is either invested in the business or you take as income to pay your mortgage, feed your family and so on. These kinds of government contracts are viewed as loss leaders by large systems integrators and consulting firms but are necessary to prise open the agency's door of greater opportunity. For the independent consultant, life is less rosy. I'm not saying don't do it but I am saying you will need to line up more than one of these engagements to keep your head above water.

Anyway, don't let the amount of time you will need to do interviews, analysis and modelling put you off. You will learn far more than the cost of the effort you put in. So what's in this book?

## Scope of This Book

This book is designed for anyone who needs to plan, conduct and analyse interviews, then model and present findings. As such, its scope is quite broad though there is a focus on business strategy-IT because that has been my personal experience. The chapters are organised in a logical sequence.

Chapter 1 is about planning. It will provide you with a global checklist for planning your project and organising your interviews.

Chapter 2 provides a specific checklist that can be used for planning each interview. This chapter introduces our case study, a strategic initiative that we will use in the following chapters.

Chapter 3 is about the interview itself: what to say during an interview and how to conduct it in order to get the most out of it. The approach taken is a goal-driven interview approach to gathering business goals for a strategic implementation.

Chapter 4 provides you tools for analysis of interview feedback and presents them in the context of the case introduced earlier.

Chapter 5 presents ways to create strategic models: goal models and contextual or ownership models using the case study as the example.

Chapter 6 provides an example of how you may wish to document and report upon your findings to your management, client or executive sponsors, from one-page feedback, to reports and presentations.

The book concludes with a summary 19-point checklist of key things to remember.

# Chapter 1
# The Plan

Why should you plan your interviews? If you don't plan, your interviews can only go wrong. You simply would not know if they went well or not because, without a plan, you would have no idea of what you needed to find out. Without a plan, you won't be able to manage an interview or the interviewee. Before we look at the individual interview, we first need to know more about the project itself.

## The Project Checklist

In order to plan for a set of interviews you should prepare answers to the questions/tasks you need to do as listed in Table 1.1. The project preparation checklist forms the structure of the plan. To complete the plan, you answer the questions and document the answers, where appropriate. Once all the necessary questions have been answered, you can then feel even more confident about conducting a set of interviews.

Though there are many questions in Table 1.1, it isn't always the case that you will need to consider all of these. You may need to only use some. You may also want to address alternatives to these by adding to or deleting questions. Please feel free to do so. Though what I am suggesting is a fairly comprehensive approach, I expect you to be flexible and only use what is useful and relevant to your context. The columns in the table are self-explanatory. 'Answer?' is for answers to questions when needed. Ensure you list the person responsible for the activity. This allows you to cross check and confirm. If you're the only interviewer, then you can ignore this column. Except, of course, there are activities in the list that might be the responsibility of the client. If you know who is responsible for organising interviews, for instance, add their name and contact details such as a phone number and email. The 'Issues' column is a place where you can very briefly highlight any concerns over the specific planning activity. This then acts as a reminder that you need to resolve the issue. It's easy to forget the plan once you dive into the actual interview work. Reminders really help so make use of them.

Remember this is a checklist for *planning* the interviews. Once you've completed the plan, you have to be able to conduct the interviews and that involves further planning, as described in Chapter 2. For now, though, let's get on with the preparation, starting with the first item in Table 1.1.

**Table 1.1**     **Project preparation checklist**

| # | Item | Answer? | Responsible and Contact | Issues |
|---|------|---------|-------------------------|--------|
| 1 | What is the overriding objective for the engagement? | To ensure the proposed infrastructure meets needs of business units across organisation | Me and acting CIO (email/phone) | Actual CIO returns in two months and is already voicing a different opinion |
| 2 | What is the context of the engagement? | ABC123 are embarking on a technology refresh as their current infrastructure is beginning to show cracks [see attachment 2 for more detail] | Me and acting CIO | None – time frame short but can be done if work commences in one week (date) |
| 3 | Who are you going to interview? | See list attached | ... | ... |
| 4 | Who are the high-priority interviewees? | See list attached | | |
| 5 | In what order should you interview people? | | | |
| 6 | When should the interview happen? | | | |
| 7 | Where should the interview take place? | | | |
| 8 | What equipment should you take into an interview? | | | |
| 9 | Who arranges the interviews? | | | |
| 10 | What is an optimal number of interviews for your engagement? | | | |

| # | Item | Answer? | Responsible and Contact | Issues |
|---|------|---------|-------------------------|--------|
| 11 | How long do you have to do the interviews? | | | |
| 12 | Will there by follow ups/feedback? | | | |
| 13 | How many interviewers do you need? | | | |
| 14 | Are there special instructions from your client about the interview plan or subsequent phases? | | | |

## WHAT IS THE OVERRIDING OBJECTIVE FOR THE PROJECT?[1]

Normally there is one overarching goal for an engagement. It's like a Vision statement for your project. You need to find out what it is. This objective might vary from stakeholder to stakeholder but there will be a single stakeholder with overall authority for your engagement, its execution and outcomes. Why do you need to know about this? Surely you're hired to just find out about stuff? Well, yes in the most abstract sense, you are. But in order to bring a sense of purpose to your own work and steer the project in the right direction, knowing the point of your engagement helps. It helps in determining what elements of the following to focus on:

- context of engagement;

- scope of deliverable;

- range of stakeholders to interview;

- expectation of your client on what you will deliver.

Some examples of overriding objectives:

- identify gaps in current supply chain business processes and propose mechanisms for plugging gaps;

---

1   I use the terms 'project' and 'engagement' interchangeably – read them as meaning the same thing. Engagement is used more if you are a consultant and project if you are an in-house BA.

- establish root causes for critical release failures and identify potential short and longer-term solutions;

- show how new infrastructure provides business benefits across the organisation;

- gauge public sector reaction to product 'y' claims.

Note that the examples are not mission or operational statements – they say nothing about how you go about the engagement, only what you are trying to achieve. Also note that the first two are in two halves:

1.    identify/establish current situation of 'x', whatever 'x' is;

2.    propose solutions to solve/redress problem in (1).

It is important that these statements push you towards a well-scoped deliverable. The final two examples simply push for well-scoped deliverables of a known phenomenon.

## WHAT IS THE CONTEXT OF THE ENGAGEMENT?

Finding out the context of the engagement is very important. If you can get some grounding in the context, this will put you on a good footing with your prospective client/colleagues. You will be able to discuss the broad goals of the engagement with reference to the background context. This will give you a good sense of the scope of the engagement. It will importantly give your client a feeling of confidence that you are the right person for the job.

Context does not grow on trees so you need to do some initial research. Of course, you won't do this until you know you are potentially going to be engaged on the project. Typically, you'll be contacted by a stakeholder who is involved in the project or by reference from a friend or interested party who introduces you to the prospective client. You will quickly learn something about the engagement from this first contact:

- Who the client is and what the client's company does.

- The type of engagement, for example: aligning strategy, gathering requirements, post mortem review, mid-term review, requirements validation, market analysis and so on. You'll also need to find out about geography – do you need to travel between sites and even cities?

- The scale of the engagement – roughly how big it is, that is, how much money has gone into the project, how long is it expected to run/how long did it run for?

- The importance of the project to the client – is it strategic?

- What is the potential impact/was the actual impact of the project?

- What does the client expect from you?

- What are the time frames for delivery?

If you are working in-house, then you should already know about the project you are going to work on prior to being called in. That means you need to keep up with what your company is doing, especially if it is a large project. The last thing you want to happen is for a senior manager to call you in and ask you to get some information together about 'project x' and for you to reply 'what's project x?' when it has been in every internal memo for the last six months!

How do you find out about your client? This will depend on your client. If the client is a publicly listed company or government agency, then you can find out a lot of information from the annual reports that it has to make publicly available every year. But why should you bother with this? Understanding your client's business is important because it will allow you to understand its current health – is the company booming or struggling? This will tell you something about:

- the working environment to expect;

- how motivated and stressed out the people you will interview are going to be; and

- the importance the client places on the project and your engagement.

If the company is private it will be most unlikely it publishes any financial information. But it should have a website and this will give you a good idea of the business the client is in, the products and/or services it offers and also who's running the company. You should check these people out because this will give you a feel for the culture of the company. Does the chief executive officer (CEO) have a proven track record in the other companies he has worked in? What about the chief information officer (CIO)? This will tell you about the current state of your client's company in terms of drive to succeed in its market. Who are its customers? If your client is government then it is often harder to find out about the agency culture and its effectiveness, unless you are an insider in government yourself. But at least all government agencies have a mountain of freely available information about themselves, often including a strategic plan. You should always take a look at this to get an idea of what the agency is trying to achieve and how it plans to do it.

Ask around. Do you know someone who worked in/knows about your client's business/project/product? What is their experience/knowledge? If you are in-house, do you know someone working on the project? What is their impression?

Get the client to provide you background documents on the engagement. If you are being asked to do a feasibility study, ask about whether there is a marketing/business plan you can read. Is there a business case? Are there any corporate brochures, slideware presentations to look at? If you are being engaged to interview stakeholders as part of a post mortem review, ask for any project documents the client is prepared to hand over. Were there any major incidents? What were they? Did they make the press? Some do. The documents might not always be appropriate but they give you some context and get you to start thinking about the engagement.

## SCENARIO: HOW A JAPANESE COMPANY WORKS WITH ITS CLIENT

A leading Japanese systems integration (SI) company, Nomura Research Institute (NRI), before commencing an engagement, and at its own expense, sends a team of consultants into the client company to read up as much information as possible on the client and project at hand for a week prior to starting the work proper. Effectively, NRI is learning about the context of the engagement before getting too deeply into it so that: (1) NRI consultants understand the language and landscape of their client's business; (2) NRI appears as it truly is – highly professional; and (3) it delivers real value from day one.

## CONTEXT CHECKLIST

Table 1.2 lists the key things you should consider when thinking about context. Remember that working through one of these tables doesn't mean background reading is over. All it means is you've done some homework and are reading up in order to present a knowledgeable face to a nice suit. It may not sound like a lot but it means a great deal to a client when you can talk their business from the start, even if it is only in terms of generalities. The specifics are what you will find once you get your hands on some of the documents not made public and of course when you start interviewing.

**Table 1.2    Context checklist**

| # | Context Description | Key Points | Source |
|---|---|---|---|
| 1 | Client | Type of organisation<br>Market<br>Market position<br>Leading products<br>Vision and key strategies<br>History of organisation<br>Management | Annual reports<br>Company website<br>Personal contacts<br>Client brochures |
| 2 | Type of engagement | Size of project<br>Size/impact of disaster<br>Number of<br>anticipated interviews | Sponsor in<br>client organisation<br>Point of contact in<br>client organisation<br>Go-between (match maker)<br>Press |
| 3 | Expectations | Time frames<br>Deliverables<br>Importance – who will<br>see report?<br>Chain of command – your<br>reporting line back to the<br>client and the client's hand<br>that feeds you | Sponsor in<br>client organisation<br>Point of contact in<br>client organisation<br>Go-between (match maker) |
| 4 | Culture | Anticipated mood of client<br>Anticipated mood of project | Company reports<br>Press<br>Word of mouth |
| 5 | Your thinking/impressions | Working environment<br>Team required<br>Time frames you<br>can manage<br>Costs<br>Notional idea of total fee<br>Engagement structure | All of the above |

Note entry point 5 in Table 1.2 above: 'Your thinking/impressions'. This is really important so I've left it to last. You will form an opinion even if you don't want to. You will need to go into the engagement with some pre-conceived ideas about the company and the engagement itself. Why? Surely this would be a bad thing and you might even embarrass yourself? Well, no, not really. You might ask a dumb question but the point is you *do* ask the question. This will get a response and you will get an answer that will provide you with more accurate context and scope to the engagement's overriding objective. You will learn more if you ask. And you must always learn as much as possible. Also, if you have a team that is going to conduct the engagement, then you should get together with team members to thrash out your thinking about the type of engagement, what you know about the client and what you might expect. You will probably find your first impressions are wrong to some extent, but you need to start somewhere so start now. For now, though, let's get back to the planning.

## WHO ARE YOU GOING TO INTERVIEW?

This decision is often made for you. Typically your client will have a prepared list of relevant stakeholders for you to interview. But just because you have a list does not mean you should stick religiously to it. There is nothing wrong with deviating from the list provided you have good cause, such as a key stakeholder was accidently excluded, or you needed a second opinion from a specific job role. You'll find that the list may have missed somebody out because the person or persons who prepared the list of interviewees were unaware of who all the major players are.

The important thing to remember about who you interview is to cover all the key roles or aspects of the project. If you are engaged on a Strategic IT project, you will need to interview:

- C-level management. There are few C-level employees and most are far too busy to see you. But you should at least talk with the CIO. The CIO might even be your client. Ask about the business, the strategy, the IT.

- General managers/division heads. Many will be are affected by the proposed system or the newly installed system. Ask about: how each division/business unit interprets and meets the corporate strategy; about the division's business; about the impact of IT on that business; the role of IT in delivering that business.

- Programme/portfolio managers. Strategic projects are often part of a larger programme of work. There will be a programme manager/portfolio manager who oversees all the projects for that programme or portfolio. Ask about how the programme meets the strategy and how the engagement project fits into the programme. What are the project's dependencies with other projects? What are the affected business processes?

- IT team members. An enterprise architect will have some understanding of the business organisation and strategy and will know a lot about the IT infrastructure. Ask what's new/needed/changed? How will that be managed/was that managed? How was change handled?

- IT team members. A project manager can give you the overview of the project and hopefully where it fits into the bigger programme picture. What's the critical path for the project? What are the high-priority requirements? Where is the project being delayed?

- IT team members. Who else? What about the business analyst (BA), who is the conduit between business and IT? Who does the BA think is really key to talk to? How is the IT going to help deliver on the strategy? If you're investigating an IT failure, talk to developers, talk to designers, talk to infrastructure managers. If you're the BA, you shouldn't interview yourself, of course!

- Customers. Customers could be citizens, such as those who use a government website to claim benefits. Ask questions like: What's the impact on citizens of the change from face-to-face meetings to using a website? Did the website provide all the information you needed? Did it work? What advice did you get if you were stuck? What do you need to be able to do? Did you have easy access to a computer with internet connectivity?

- Users are similar to customers and more likely to be internal to the organisation. Users use the software that's built to help do their jobs, such as input data, produce management reports, interact with customers. Don't talk to every single user unless there are less than 10 but do talk to representatives for each of the different roles. Ask questions like: What does your job entail? Does the system allow you to do all you wanted to do with the system? What are the workarounds? How do you fix them? What do you do in your job? How does the system positively/negatively impact your job? Walk me through a typical transaction.

For a post mortem review of a major project failure of an external public release, such as customer-facing systems shutting down in offices where customers renew passports because of a bug in the printer queuing software, you should probably talk to:

- All roles listed above.

- Customers (again). How did the failure affect them? What could they/couldn't they now do? Don't talk to every customer but if there is a customer representative group of some kind, go have a conversation.

- Incident report managers. Who records the incident? What happens to the report? What is the process? What is the reporting line?

- Customer office managers. How did they handle the shut down/ crash/disaster? What were the workarounds? What were their teams informed about before, during and/or after the incident?

- IT architects. Find out how the printing bug got into the system.

- Quality Assurance. How did the print bug get through the testing process?

As I said at the start of this section, who you talk to is largely predetermined before you step into the room. The above examples give you an idea of the roles you want to think about interviewing. It is not an exhaustive or all-inclusive list. You may need to talk to a more diverse range of roles. You may only get to talk to half the number you really needed to interview.

On some occasions you may find yourself presented with a handful of key people to interview but then are left to your own devices about whom else to talk to. When you're working on strategic projects you may be able to call upon the organisational chart to find out who is in what role, though more often than not, roles and responsibilities are delegated irrespective of official job title so you will have to find out.[2] Ask the interviewees you've spoken to, your sponsor and point of contact. But be aware of your client's expectations and your own on:

- delivery time frame;

- cost;

- when enough is enough.

The first two points are obvious. You will have agreed a deliverable deadline with your client so you should aim to stick to it. You should think about the cost to yourself of conducting unanticipated and therefore unplanned and unbudgeted interviews. Do you have staff available? Do you have other engagements after this one already agreed? Also, the cost to your client: you can't at this point revise your contractual agreement very easily – I wish you luck if you try! – and any further delay in receiving your report might hurt your client's reputation as well as yours. That's a place you want to avoid ending up in. In a nutshell, you will cost your engagement, establish a fee and get this approved mostly before the engagement commences. You base the cost, in part, on number of interviewees, so you need to build in a bit of slack to pay for the extra interviews that always seem to materialise once you're up and running. If you're an in-house BA, your project manager still has to factor all of the above into the project costs and schedule.

Remember from the Introduction where I list out how long it will take to conduct interviews? You will know very quickly into an engagement what your time frame for delivery is if you didn't know at the start. If you keep adding more clients to interview, you'll push back the delivery and pile more work onto your plate. Deciding when enough is enough is not easy because you need to convince your client you've been of value.

Quick note: if you're a researcher or a student and have taken a look at this list you might start to wonder about the relevance to what it is you're researching or studying. This is something to think about. The point I am making above is that you need to think about whom you will interview in more detail than you might have assumed. You need to place that interviewee in the context of the engagement and ask appropriate questions about the right topic in the right context.

---

2   At one engagement I worked on, the client's organisational chart for Senior Executives was updated on a monthly basis. Though staff were often rebadged their roles remained the same, and others were rebranded though their titles remained unaltered. It was a confusing place to work at from time to time.

## WHO ARE THE HIGH-PRIORITY INTERVIEWEES?

You will be aware that some people speak with more authority than others; this is because they simply know more, shout louder and/or are in a higher and more responsible position. When you are interviewing a large number of people you will have to ultimately put some weight into who these high-priority people are and what they do in the company, or whether they are leading experts, meaning that you have to set some stock in their authority. If your engagement is to model a strategy and business process optimisation, then you would add more weight to the interviewees who happen to be the chief strategy officer and assorted business process owners than an IT project manager. Conversely, you would put more weight onto what a project manager tells you about the IT team's current workload than the chief strategy officer.

Some things to consider when prioritising interviewees:

- What is the scope of the context of the project you are engaged on? This will help you decide which interviewees are in scope and how central those interviewees are to the problem and solution.

- Did the system you are reviewing affect customers, end users, suppliers, the bottom line? Getting a handle on the impact will give you a good idea of key players. For example, if end customers were affected badly, then it would be important to talk with a customer representative and, if that is not possible, talk with front line staff. Their experiences will be most valuable to keep in mind because, ultimately, your client wants to keep its customers happy and as a consequence its staff happy.

- Is your client's new product targeted at retirees, at middle-income earners, at teenagers, at cats? You won't be able to interview the cats but you should consider talking with cat owners as a high priority, perhaps the highest.

- Have all roles been taken into consideration when arranging interviews? That is, did your client forget to mention the 30,000 casual users of the library system that just happen to be external to the organisation the library sits in but form the biggest user demographic? He might have. But how do you get to talk to these casual users?

It's not easy to prioritise stakeholders until you can get a good understanding of the context of the engagement. Even then, you'll find yourself giving more emphasis to the most eloquent and lucid interviewee even though his role suggests he is not in a position to speak authoritatively on any number of key issues. There is a danger that you put too much weight in this interviewee only because the interview went so smoothly and was a welcome relief from the previous interviews.

If you are eliciting requirements for an IT system, prioritisation of stakeholders is a little different in that you will actually categorise into types of stakeholders, such as data entry clerks, client representatives, managers, help desk staff, customers. Each group will have different sets of requirements (of which some may overlap) and then these requirements will need prioritising so you'll spend much more of your time prioritising requirements than stakeholders.

You might put most weight behind the highest-ranking staff member you spoke to. If you spoke to the CEO then surely everything he said was the truth and the definitive word on the matter? Well, yes in some things that's true, for instance in the competitive strategy the company is supposed to take. But the CEO won't be the expert on how that strategy is executed across all business lines. You'll have to give weight to the division managers or general managers or process owners for that. The CEO won't know how IT is going to be most effectively used in supporting the business process. The CIO might know something about that, as well as members of his staff and those divisional and general managers. The manager of the users of the IT will know something about that too. The users themselves can tell you something important as well.

The point here is there is no hard and fast formula for prioritising the importance of interviewees. It is context dependent. Context is everything. Without context you are in a vacuum and there's not much room to breathe in one of those.

## IN WHAT ORDER ARE YOU GOING TO INTERVIEW PEOPLE?

Top down. If it is at all possible for you to organise the order of your interviews, do it top down. Start with the senior management and work down the ladder, ending up with the operational people. That's the theory and, if you can execute it, it works best. More often than not, however, you will find that interviews have already been arranged so you will not be able to influence the schedule. Also, the more senior staff will be booked up and therefore harder to get time with than operational staff. So you may well be confronted with many more middle-to-operational staff to interview first than you might initially have wished for.

Why does this matter? You're going to interview them all anyway aren't you? Well, yes, you are. But the idea behind top down is:

1.     How much detail can you handle immediately? Operational staff will typically give you mountains of localised information.

2.     Can you put all that minute detail into the right context without a good grasp of the overall context to start with?

Interviewing senior management first will give you a better idea of the bigger picture and the wider context for the engagement, of the project, of its impact. This will put you in good stead to gradually drill down to the detail.

Of course, the context of the engagement will help you determine in what order you interview people – *if* you get a choice. If you are conducting a post mortem review that left customers unable to make benefit claims because of a website failure and that left them out of pocket and unable to pay their bills, you would probably want to know about this impact before trying to work out what went wrong technically. That would allow you to put into perspective the very technical context you will no doubt elicit. So you would want to talk to one or more customer representatives and representatives of the front line staff dealing with customers face-to-face on a daily basis. But you would do this only after talking with a senior manager about the website in general and what services it provides. You would also want to talk to senior management about the impact across the benefits agency and beyond. After that, you would then turn to the details of the reporting process, the incident response team, the service desk. Only then would you ideally want to talk to various IT staff. Getting the IT team to tell you all their woes prior to an understanding of what went wrong in terms of impact on the individual customers and the organisation as a whole can give you a confused and murky picture. You need your reference point of light before you head into the darkness.

Yet again, context dictates. But so does your client in the majority of cases because those senior staff and often the front line staff are less readily available than other internal operational staff such as the IT team. All you can do is try to influence your client to get the interviews in as good an order as possible, or wrestle control away from the administrator who is arranging interviews so that you can do it yourself. The risk is that you will delay the engagement deliverable because, as I said, the more senior the staff member, the harder to pin down. And you don't want to delay unnecessarily. This means though you'd rather be top down, you're more likely to end bottom up or at best middle out.

Two notes of caution:

1. Do not work your way down the organisational chart in its precise order! In other words, do not begin with the CEO, and only then the chief operations officer (COO), and only then the chief financial officer (CFO), and only then the CIO and so on. If you get the opportunity to interview a division head, a general manager, the chief technology officer (CTO), before interviewing the CEO, then do it. An executive manager is after all an executive manager, will know the strategy and will be an excellent guide in getting the bigger picture.

2. If by any chance or good luck you do manage to land the CEO first in a big organisation – and you are more likely to win the lottery than do this – then make sure you know your context. Know the context of the business, of the project, of the company's customers. You place yourself in great danger of looking like what you are, an unordained outsider, if you haven't done your preparation. That's why it's better, and far more likely, to arrange an interview with another senior executive or two prior to meeting the CEO.

## WHEN SHOULD THE INTERVIEW HAPPEN?

Are there better days of the week to hold interviews? Are there better times of day than others? My take on this is that you are there to do a job so you'd better get those interviews done as quickly as possible and hope you are not too disruptive. But as you're in the client's face you are already a disruption. You will have to be flexible. You will have to adapt. You will have to insist on interviewing people even when inconvenient if that is what it takes to get the job done. You *will* be interviewing people on Monday morning at 8 a.m. when no one else is in the office. You might even get to interview someone on Friday afternoon when all hell has already broken loose in the mad rush to get a product up live before closing time. Under these circumstances be aware that your interviewee is going to be stressed, even panicking, distracted, fiddling with his mobile or pager and frantically glancing at the door in case his manager bursts in screaming to get back to the boiler room.

My advice in these situations: be proactive. If you know a deadline is fast approaching and the whole IT team has booked into the hotel across the street readying for an all-night assault to get the product out live before the New York Stock Exchange starts trading, then postpone all planned interviews for that Friday and probably for a few days before it. Reschedule. Inform your client of your intention first. Make sure they clear this – they will probably be very grateful for letting them get on with their jobs. Ensure all interviewees are aware of the reschedule and the planned appointments for the following week. Tell them individually if you can, send an email, make a phone call, then get out of their hair. Head back to your office and work on something else for a few days, like writing up what you've already done.

How many interviews can you conduct per day without losing your sanity? Interviewing is really exhausting. You have to be switched on the whole time. Remember you are having a conversation that goes both ways. You may only be allowed to take handwritten notes or want to check recordings against your notes. So you have to process what was just said in your mind, summarise it and write it down, *and* keep listening as the interviewee keeps talking.

## SCENARIO: THE EXPERIENCE OF MULTIPLE INTERVIEWS IN ONE DAY

On one engagement, because of time pressures I had to interview six people in a single day and keep this up for two weeks. In all but one interview, I got permission to record it. I was primarily working with a partner who took notes, and we tag-teamed occasionally on asking questions though I played the lead interviewer. Believe me, I was completely frazzled by the fourth interview on the first day. After the third day, I was on autopilot. By the end of the week I couldn't remember anything from the interviews, couldn't write my own name and couldn't read what I had written. I found myself repeating questions, missing out others and assigning responses to the wrong interviewees – until I checked the recordings. It was a gruelling experience. On other engagements since, I have been extremely careful about scheduling.

You are often not in a position to dictate when an interview should or shouldn't occur. Mostly, the schedule is done for you before you can have much of a say. Schedules are also dictated by availability and critical business issues, such as getting that deliverable out by Friday evening. You have to take all these factors into account but if you are in a privileged position to set the schedule, be aware of when is a good time for your interviewee as well as for yourself. If you are a researcher, you may find you have more freedom to influence the schedule than if you are a consultant or BA. Use this freedom wisely, taking into account these factors and others such as whom you might wish to interview first or nearly first and where the interviews can take place.

## WHERE SHOULD THE INTERVIEW TAKE PLACE?

I have conducted interviews in all kinds of inappropriate places: the worst being a tiny, extremely busy and hence very noisy cafe in full flow at lunch time. The table my interviewee and I sat at was equally small – only room for a couple of coffee cups, no room for my notepad. I managed to record the interview but playing through it afterwards, all I had recorded was background noise with the occasional word from both myself and the interviewee. My notes were scribbled as I balanced the notepad on my knee. I was also jostled regularly by waiters squeezing through to serve a continual stream of customers trundling past us. It was not a good experience but a lesson was learned. Get the location for the interview set up appropriately.

The location matters but if you are a consultant you may not know the location options until you get on the client site. Don't hold interviews in noisy cafes or even in quiet ones unless there is no better choice. Most companies have one or two rooms that are available as meeting rooms. You are more likely to get given one of those or both. So that's pretty straightforward, right? Well, there are always a few things to consider.

### Where is the room?

This is a good first question. Do you know where to go? If you're in a large office block or have interviews at multiple sites, do you know how to get to where you are meant to be? How long does it take to get there? If you are rushing from one location to the next, do you have enough time to get there and get set up before the interview starts? How do you get to your next interview? Catch a bus/train/plane? Drive a hire car? Does it have satellite navigation? Do you have a road map if you're driving? Can you park nearby without getting a parking ticket? You will need to plan your interview schedule around these concerns: if you are driving from location to location, you will need to schedule your project in accordance. Often you don't know much about locations until you get the project rolling and the time frames have been agreed. It's not a bad idea to drop a hint about extending deadlines because of the travel requirements if this travel is going to significantly delay delivery: for instance, you've just been asked to travel to Canberra from Sydney to interview 10 key people who are themselves at five different sites spread across the Australian Capital Territory, when you were originally told interviewees would only be in Sydney in the same building. The number of planned interviews has not increased but the location change and seniority of the Canberra interviewees means a significant slippage in schedule. You might be able to arrange all the interviews over two days but it is more likely, especially if interviewees are senior management, that the interviews can only be done over a few weeks because of availability. It you take just a few extra days, I would not want to make any fuss about deadlines. Costs are another matter. This will need to be discussed because flying or driving adds significant overhead to the budget. And consultants don't travel by bus.

### Is the room too close to the place of work?

Conversely, if you are interviewing someone right next to their desk or even at their desk, there are going to be a number of potential distractions that affect the success of the interview. Colleagues are going to be within earshot for starters. You probably do not want colleagues to overhear what is being discussed because this breaks the confidential agreement you have with your interviewee. Also, colleagues may not realise a formal interview is being undertaken and will naturally wander over for a chat or to discuss some piece of work. Of course, you might well be at someone's desk in order for that person to show you something on a computer, such as how that person uses the current supply chain management system. In this case, you do need to be at the interviewee's desk. But it is a good idea once the demo is over to relocate to a more private room.

Do you need an access pass to get into the room, into the office, into the building?

Your client should arrange access for you but sometimes it can take a while and means you have to convince security at the front desk you are not an industrial spy each time you go to your client's office. Check if you need a key, then find out who has the key and if that person will be available when you need access.

### Do you need to book the room?

Almost certainly. If you're conducting a number of interviews you will be spending a lot of time in the interview room. If there is a booking system, use it, otherwise you will find yourself sitting on the steps on the fire escape. Or the local cafe. If someone is arranging time slots for interviews for you, ensure that person also books the room. If your interviews are scheduled for one every two hours on a given day, try to get the room block booked for the whole day. This room will become your operational HQ. As I said earlier in this section, often there are only one or two meeting rooms for you to operate in. These get booked up very early by staff holding regular and emergency meetings so make sure the bookings for your interviews get done quickly and as soon as dates and times have been confirmed with interviewees. If there is a real emergency on and staff need a war room, vacate as fast as you can and look for an alternative room if your interviewee is still available.

## So what does a good interview room look like?

A good room starts with a good location. So try and make sure the room is in the same office block as your interviewee's desk but on a different floor. If possible, the room should be located fairly near conveniences like toilets and a drinks area such as a kitchen or dispensing machine. But not too near because these facilities will create unwanted background noise. There should be a good-sized central desk with office chairs around it. There should be a spare chair or two because interviewees sometimes prefer to turn up in groups unannounced. The desk shape doesn't matter. Its size should be enough to easily put all your equipment on it without feeling cluttered. The interviewee should not feel crowded. Light should be good. The room should feel bright with good air flow. A good-sized window would help with that. Don't use spot lamps to burn retinas. Artificial lighting above should be bright and of the non-flicker variety. One CIO I worked with had an office in the bowels of the IT department that had no natural light source. When he complained about the lighting, an occupational health check was done. The room's lighting was changed to produce a more accommodating ambience – in theory. What he actually got was what he called his 'disco'. The lighting made his room glow orange and green looking in; looking out, the world had taken on a pale blue hue.

The room should be warm but not hot. You don't want the interviewee and/or yourself feeling sleepy. The room, conversely, should not be too cool. This will make your interviewee and you twitch and want to get out of there really fast. If you can control the air conditioning, do so. Ambience matters. Neutral wall colouring, if possible. One or two pictures are fine, not too many otherwise you'll be discussing art instead of the project.

Free space. A room that gives you and the interviewee plenty of walking space around the table is valuable. You will not feel claustrophobic or uncomfortably squashed in. There should also be a space where you can put bags, briefcases and so on without tripping over them every time you stand up.

If it is hot, arrange for a water jug and glasses to be available. Just remember that if you're interviewing several people in a row, someone, probably you, will have to wash those glasses up and replenish the water supply.

## What equipment should you take into an interview?

The layout of the room is important for comfort and to make the interviewee feel relatively relaxed but there are a number of things you need to bring to the interview to ensure all goes smoothly. Table 1.3 lists the equipment I would recommend to have at hand and why.

**Table 1.3     Equipment for interviews**

| Item | Rationale | Comments |
|---|---|---|
| Notepad | You will need to take notes even if you record. | Make sure the notepad is a good size with plenty of empty pages – you will write a lot. |
| Pens/pencils and sharpener | For making notes. | You will need several as backup. |
| Audio recording device | Capture every spoken word. | If battery operated, charge it beforehand and bring spare batteries if possible and a charger cable. Bring an extension lead. The older iPods are fantastic – you will need to buy a microphone for one. |
| Whiteboard/butcher paper flip chart, board pens, board wiper | Either you or your interviewee might want to diagram something as explanation. | Ask for a whiteboard/flip chart and pens to be available in the room. |
| Digital camera | To take a picture of what is on the whiteboard or butcher paper. | You may find that any writing is hard to read from the image or lines are faint. It is a good idea to hand copy the notes on the board as well if time permits. |
| Lap top | This is optional and depends entirely on context. If you need to show something like a software application or slides or a diagram, for example. | Bring a power cable. Check the lead is long enough to reach the power socket. Be careful where this is plugged in. You don't want to trip nor trip up the interviewee so use an extension lead. |
| Projector and screen | Optional. Show a larger image than your computer screen. You may wish to openly complete a form or make changes to a document with the help of your interviewee. | Get your client to set one up for you if the client has one. If you have one and really need it, bring the projector in. Project against a bare wall or the whiteboard if the screen is going a step too far. |

| Item | Rationale | Comments |
|------|-----------|----------|
| Clock/watch | Timing is everything. You have to know how much time you are taking during each interview. You can soon get a feel for how long an interview is going to take and can revise your question list accordingly. | Don't place a big alarm clock in the middle of the table. This will make the interviewee nervous and be distracted with the time. Be discreet. Occasionally glance at your watch. Don't use a mobile phone, switch yours off. |
| Business cards | Sometimes you want to provide contact details to interviewees. Sometimes other opportunities emerge from interviews. | Don't hand these to everyone. You may be acting as a sub-prime. That is, you may have been hired by a consulting company to work with them in doing the job. This means the consulting company may wish you to represent them rather than your own business. You might even get business cards and an email address of the consulting company that hired you. |

Do not hand business cards to all and sundry, only to those who can make a difference to you in a positive way. That is, senior managers may want to retain you for further work given their positive experience in the interview and other contact times. Your client, your point of contact and their administration should have your contact details. Use discretion about providing this to others. If you are a direct engagement with a client, the same rules apply. Be discerning about who gets a card.

Avoid projectors in interviews as much as humanly possible. You need projectors for presentations – giving information, not getting information.

If you are not going to use the lap top in the interview, make sure you keep it packed away. A cool lap top can attract attention and can clutter tables. Plus you'll probably forget about all the cables dangling dangerously at ankle height.

That's quite a lot of equipment but ultimately you only really ever need four items for interviews:

1.    notebook

2.    pens/pencils

3.    audio recording device

4.    watch/clock.

Remember to turn off your mobile phone. The reason for this is: if you begin to fiddle with your phone, your interviewee will also do the same with their mobile. This will be a distraction. If there is a clock on the wall or on a desk, organise the interview room so you can see the clock without turning your head too much. Don't keep looking at the clock either; you will only give the impression that you would rather be someplace else.

## WHO ARRANGES THE INTERVIEWS?

If you are a consultant, interviews will be mostly organised by your client at the start, as I've indicated above. If you have a long list – over 20 interviews to conduct – then you should be reasonably happy someone has taken the trouble for you. But don't expect to just roll up. The following scenario should make you think twice about sitting back and allowing someone else to do the work:

## SCENARIO: ENSURE YOU ARE AWARE OF THE INTERVIEW SCHEDULE

I once did a contract that involved a post mortem review of a software project. Arrangements for making the interview bookings were left in the hands of the client. All in, we interviewed 30-plus staff from several divisions in three weeks. But we missed some key interviews and these nearly cost us the contract. Our client had left arrangements for the interviews to a personal assistant (PA) to whom he'd provided a list of interviewees. She emailed each and informed them of when and where interviews would take place. The interviewee spreadsheet (names, roles, departments, times and location of interviews) should have been updated by the PA when interviewees replied they were unavailable and had suggested alternative time slots. This list may have been updated but the version sent to us was not. The result was we had a number of very senior staff turn up to rearranged interviews that they knew about and the PA knew about, but we didn't. On several occasions I sat with my colleague in an empty room waiting in vain. The PA had failed to provide us with the updated schedule. When we figured this out – upon receiving phone calls from angry employees – we managed to get an updated list from the PA, an updated but still out-of-date list. And so we sat in those empty rooms waiting for people who were waiting elsewhere at some other point in time. Ultimately, we got the blame for the mess – it took an effort to recover.

The moral of the story is, when you're conducting interviews make sure it's you who arranges them if you can. Interviewees often respond better to your invitation than some blurb written by your client that may or may not represent your take on what you were asked to find out. If you can't organise the interviews, make sure your schedule is the same as the current one that everyone else has. It is a good idea to ask for phone numbers and email addresses for each interviewee in advance. That way, you can get in contact prior to the scheduled interview and confirm it is still going ahead as planned.

## WHAT IS THE OPTIMAL NUMBER OF INTERVIEWS FOR YOUR ENGAGEMENT?

I get asked this a lot: 'How many interviews should I conduct on my project?' There's no absolute right or wrong answer. The one I tend to give is this: interview as many people as you and your client believe is necessary to get a fair and unbiased picture of whatever the engagement is about, ensuring you have covered all key role types and stakeholders within the agreed time frame for the engagement.

Time dictates when you need to deliver. If your delivery date is short then you should not set out to interview 50 people. If you have one month to execute and deliver, be extremely careful whom you choose or are told to interview. The Introduction explains how long it takes to plan and conduct interviews, and prepare and present feedback. Remember this when drawing up or discussing a long list of interviewees. Conversely, picking too few interviewees is ill advised even if time is short because you will not get a fair reflection. Make more time or, if that is not possible, hold a workshop where you can get a number of stakeholders in one room at the same time. As I said in the Introduction, interviewing is not the only technique available for gathering information. There are times when workshops are far more useful. If you really only have one month and 20-plus interviewees, getting them all in a room together for a day or two days will give you the coverage of your planned interviews, but may not afford the individual depth you might have liked. But you will be able to bounce ideas/thoughts off different people at the same time and this can be beneficial.[3] Remember good enough *is* good enough, yet strive for perfection. But remember to deliver a result! The other decisive factor in determining the number of interviews is the budget your client has set aside for the engagement versus your normal costing model. You'll probably find you charge more nominally than the client is willing to pay. Try to find out what kind of budget the client has in mind before committing to a large number of interviews. You need to use discretion and diplomacy here and be prepared to earn a lower fee than your costing model allows. So long as you are not losing money, you should be fine. Put it this way, is it worth taking a small loss –

---

3   A good book on running workshops is by Ellen Gottesdiener, *Requirements by Collaboration: Workshops for Defining Needs*, Boston, MA, Addison-Wesley 2002.

assuming you can still pay your bills – in order to get the subsequent, larger and vastly profitable job of overseeing the roll out of the recommendations for change that is your deliverable for this engagement?

## HOW LONG DO YOU HAVE TO DO THE INTERVIEWS?

I would only ever allow one hour for an interview, irrespective of who you are interviewing. There are reasons for this:

- How will you get through those 30 interviews in two weeks if each one runs on for two or more hours? Remember, doing an interview is not only sitting in a room and asking questions. Doing an interview involves careful planning, especially in understanding context in order to ask the right questions, then conducting the interview, and analysis, modelling and feedback presentation.

- You will burn out. It is hard to follow interviews for very long. Your mind can wander aimlessly if you have no time frame.

- Your interviewee will feel exhausted. You do not want to turn your interviewee into a zombie. He will ramble in any which direction and will not give his manager and colleagues a good report of the interview experience. The interviewee will also feel as if this is an interrogation if there is an incessant barrage of questions.

- Your interviewee is busy and will probably have to get back to the daily grind to reach the week's targets.

- If you can't find out what you want in an hour, then you're asking the wrong questions or talking to the wrong person.

- Information overload. You will get so much information from well-planned and well-run interviews of one-hour duration that you will simply not need or be able to manage anything more post that hour.

- If you find yourself overrunning, stop the interview. If you really have to, schedule a follow up.

There are exceptions: if the interviewee is the CEO or C-level or one of the most critical stakeholders who is the least available, when the hour is up begin to wind down and summarise, getting verification of what was said. Do this from memory if possible rather than poring over notes. Do not go to your recording. This interviewee mostly likely can ill afford the extra time with you anyway.

Ultimately, the decision to keep interviews to an hour or to let them run longer is yours. It comes down to a business decision: time and money. If you are a consultant you want to do the best job you can every time. But there's a limit to your time because there's a limit to your bank balance. If you're a researcher, you must consider time as critical as well in delivery of your research report or thesis. Interviewing comes down to good planning, putting in the upfront effort, doing effective and quick analysis and presenting results clearly. If you fail to get any one of these things right, the whole engagement goes out the window.

## WILL THERE BE FOLLOW UPS/FEEDBACK?

A follow up is essentially a short interview/email to confirm some facts or to expand on a question that had not been answered to your satisfaction or a new train of thought. Feedback is a written one-page summary, in bullet point format, of the interview findings that you send to or show the interviewee for confirmation. Feedback can also be findings thus far from a group of interviews with your client or team.

You should just keep in mind that you will have to provide feedback to some interviewees for validation purposes and also to follow up on anything you missed. Whether you do this for all interviewees is doubtful unless all are senior and critical to the successful outcome of the engagement. Feedback takes time; make sure that time is used wisely.

## HOW MANY INTERVIEWERS DO YOU NEED?

I recommend two: one interviewer to take notes and ask the occasional question or ask for clarity on a point, the other to ask the majority of questions. Running the whole show on your own is exhausting but can be done. The good thing with two interviewers is that one can look at emotional response and note it. If you are asking sensitive questions, it is important to capture the physical response almost as much as the verbal. Don't video the interview whatever you do, unless you're a police officer or you are conducting a research project into the use of video in interviews. Also, if you have an equipment failure such as your recording device decides to switch itself off, the second interviewer can work to fix the problem as you continue the interview.

## SCENARIO: TWO INTERVIEWEES SEE AND HEAR DIFFERENT THINGS

I was with a colleague in Japan, talking with a group of staff from NTT Data. My colleague spoke in Japanese and was making a slide presentation, also in Japanese. I do not speak Japanese but emotional reactions are similar the world over. So to play a part, I documented emotional reactions and noted them against the slide number, although I was uncertain what the slide said. After the meeting I presented my notes to my colleague. He had not been aware of the emotional response, only the verbal. Combining the emotional response with the verbal gave us a much clearer picture of what the Japanese colleagues really thought about our presentation.

You can tag team interviews but it is better that there is a definite lead interviewer. Working in tandem means you can take turns to run whole interviews though. This helps both you and your colleague because you can learn from each other's approaches and mistakes, sharpening your skills along the way.

A partner can also pull the interview back on course if it looks like it might overrun or has gone off course.

Two heads are better than one when doing the analysis. You can cross check to ensure you are making the same sense of an interview as your partner does.

## ARE THERE SPECIAL INSTRUCTIONS FROM YOUR CLIENT ABOUT THE INTERVIEW PLAN OR SUBSEQUENT PHASES?

I have been in a number of situations where my client has requested to look at the interview questions prior to conducting the interviews. In one sense this is great news because it forces you to really think about what you want to ask and what you want to find out. In another sense, your client is giving himself tacit approval about you – in other words, he is checking you out. In yet another sense, your client will offer you advice on what to ask and to whom. In the latter case, it is wise to ask any questions the client suggests, so long as they make sense to you, because you will have to feed results back to your client anyway.

What should you do if your client decides to make wholesale changes to your questions or recommends you should not ask a large percentage of them? If this happens, it's for a number of possible reasons:

- you have not done enough background research to ask the right questions;

- perhaps your client wants to find out something that you were unaware of that you should really have been aware of;

- perhaps your client is simply emphasising something that you knew about but hadn't considered important enough – your client is telling you this *is* important;

- perhaps the entire scope of the engagement has changed and you should change the scope of your questions accordingly;

- perhaps your client doesn't know what he wants.

The smart thing for you to do is to open a dialogue with your client to find out why they are making changes. If it is because of the first reason above, then you're in trouble. You should have planned better. Your client is giving you an opportunity to redeem yourself, so take it.

If the scope of the engagement is now entirely different, you will need to reassess how many people you are going to interview, who they are and when you need to have answers by. If you're a consultant you may need to rethink the terms of your contract, though, in most cases you may just have to live with less of a profit, if you can. Clients change their minds all the time and every single engagement I have had, except for the most tiny, I have had to interview many more people than originally planned. But you should always plan for more interviews than you planned in your cost estimates. Why? Because at the end of every interview you are going to ask this question: Who else do you recommend I talk to?

Many of those recommendations will be on your list of interviewees but there is always someone else who isn't. Sometimes that someone else will tell you nothing. At other times, that someone else is *the* key stakeholder. Of course, you need to follow up that one question with: Do you have (recommended person's) contact details?

You can normally find this out yourself but the best way to get people to willingly commit to an interview and speak openly is for one of their colleagues, who has already been interviewed, to set the interview up for you.

## SCENARIO: ASKING 'WHO SHOULD I TALK TO NEXT?' IS VITAL

My team was engaged to conduct a review of a requirements document for an information system in an R&D division of a company. The information system was intended to keep facts about people who were associated to the R&D division and generate reports on those numbers. The reports went to the Board and to the company's major investors. The investors required this information in order to determine: (1) the success of the associate programme; and (2) the level of investment required each financial year. The company had over 700 staff but did not know how many associates it had. The company's CIO called in my team to look at what he considered an excessively long and confusing requirements document that an internal BA had put together for the information system.

We conducted interviews with all the stakeholders whom the BA had interviewed. We established there were conflicting requirements, processes impossible to implement and many unnecessary requirements. What we also discovered was that the *key* stakeholder who was responsible for drafting the reports for the Board and the company's investors had not only not been interviewed but was also unaware a system was being proposed. This stakeholder was very senior in the organisation but worked in a different business unit at a different location. Once we'd interviewed him, it became very obvious that the vast majority of the proposed system was the fantasy of one of the other stakeholders and not relevant at all. We made our recommendations to the CIO, effectively cutting the estimated cost of the system by half.

We only found out about the key stakeholder because we asked in one interview, 'Who else do you recommend we talk to?' The interviewee had responded, 'Oh, why not talk to xxx, I think he might know something about this.' Turns out he knew everything about the reports because he was the primary reporter but knew nothing about the proposed system.

## Planning for Each Interview

Having a good idea about the context of the engagement and knowing when you are meeting your interviewees is important. But then walking in with no further preparation becomes a problem. You need to know how to handle each interview as it comes along. This is where the specific interview preparation checklist comes into play, as shown in Table 1.4.

**Table 1.4    Specific interview preparation checklist**

| Interviewee: | | Interviewer: |
|---|---|---|
| Location: | | |
| Time: | Date: | |

| # | Item | Answers? |
|---|---|---|
| 1 | What are the key objectives for each interview? | |
| 2 | What is the specific context for each interview? | |
| 3 | What questions are you going to ask? | |
| 4 | Who do you choose to follow up with? | |
| 5 | What promises can you make to an interviewee? | |
| 6 | Modifying the plan as you learn more. | |

## WHAT ARE THE KEY OBJECTIVES FOR EACH INTERVIEW?

Objectives are tied to context by a gorgon knot so it is impossible to set objectives without some consideration of context and vice versa. This means you should consider this point (1) with that of point (2) immediately below as essentially two halves of the same coin.

Before you conduct an interview, you should already know something about your engagement's overriding objective, the context for the engagement and have some background on who you are interviewing. Some straightforward questions have been presented above that you should always ask given the context of the engagement. In other words, if you ask an executive about the features of a software system used in his division by his employees, he may not even know the system exists. Ask questions at the appropriate level. Before you can establish the specific questions, you need a list of key objectives you want to achieve from each interview. They may only become clear as you get closer to the actual interview and have learned much more from prior interviews and ongoing contextual reading.

If you're interviewing an executive who has been put in charge of fixing and re-releasing a key product that failed when all printers shut down in its 200 offices, cost the company millions plus gave its reputation a very large dent, you might set these interview objectives:

1.    Establish the depth and breadth of impact of the printer failure on the business – to cross reference with what you already know from background reading and other interviews.

2.    Find out the strategy for resolving printer failure to ensure there is not a repeat.

3.    Find out the strategy for re-establishing the company's public profile and reputation.

You will have noted that the objectives address business and strategy even in reference to an essentially technical failure. That's because the executive may not be aware, understand or even care about the details of the technology other than at a superficial level – the printers stopped working in 200 offices because there was a software bug. There's no point in asking an executive about the details of a software bug in the printer drivers. You need to think strategically when working with executives.

When working with operational and engineering staff, you will need to think differently again. For these staff, your objectives will be more concrete. Examples are shown when introducing the case studies below.

## WHAT IS THE SPECIFIC CONTEXT FOR EACH INTERVIEW?

Though you are aware of the overall context for the engagement, such as a new system has been proposed or a leading product failed on its global release, you should establish the context for each interview. This will validate specific interview objectives you have set. In other words, given you are interviewing a technical manager, the context or scope of the interview ought to consider the technical aspects of the new product or release failure, looking at impact on the operational aspects of the business. If you are interviewing an executive, your context will be broader and you might only get a broad brush of the business or a key process cutting across business units. Ensure you scope your interview questions to address both the objectives and the context so that they are relevant and poignant to the interviewee. Examples are shown when introducing the case study in Chapter 2.

## Summary

This chapter has discussed at length how important it is to plan for an interview and even for a commercial engagement with a client, and what to do to get the planning right. What is needed now is to work on what specific questions to ask. This is discussed in the following chapter.

# Chapter 2

# What Questions Are You Going to Ask?

This is the $64,000 dollar question: What do you ask when you interview someone? Absolutely the worst thing you can do is walk into an interview and have no idea what to ask. Just relying upon the interviewee to 'tell you all about it' is a recipe for failure. In a more specific IT context, if you're the BA, walk into an interview and ask, 'So tell me what your requirements are?' you're not going to get much of an answer – most of the time! So you should consider these points when deciding on the key set of questions:

- Why were you hired? That is, what was the brief, the overriding objective?

- Who are you going to be interviewing? Pitching your questions at the right level is critical.

- What have you discovered from doing your homework that's relevant to this specific interview and needs verification? What did you find out about the customer, the project and the people on it through your own investigation prior to commencing the interviews and from the interviews and analysis already done?

Remember the example scenario of NRI putting in a team of consultants to learn about its client's context in Chapter 1? You are unlikely to be able to afford this luxury so you'll need to find another way to do this. Often you as the consultant or researcher will have to do all the work yourself. And do it you must.

## SCENARIO: YOU DON'T NEED A LONG LIST OF QUESTIONS

In one of my very first engagements as an analyst, on a project to re-engineer a business process and supporting inventory management system, I conducted a number of interviews with both management and operational staff. I planned the interviews meticulously, using what texts I could find and seeking advice from experts. Trouble was, I was overambitious in what information I could collect in the one-hour slot designated per interview. I had a very long list of 20 questions for each interview – there were about a dozen interviews in all – and I stuck relentlessly to those questions, too naive to deviate or skip or rephrase. As a result, each interview went on for two hours or more. The interviewees were generous enough to give me the time, but looking back, this was a ridiculous situation. I was also on my own and had decided to simply write down the answers verbatim as the interviewees spoke. So I kept interrupting them in full flow and asked them to repeat what they said. Looking back, I had far too many questions and failed to manage the time well.

Always commence an interview by saying to the interviewee: 'Tell me about your business/your job/role.' This will put the interviewee at ease and give you the best guide to the context that interviewee inhabits almost immediately. You can move on to more specific questions after that.

## Questions: The Five Ws and One H

There are some basic questions you can ask that revolve around the five Ws: why, what, where, when and who; and the one H: how. These need to be tailored to the role your interviewee fills. For instance, if you are interviewing the CEO of a company, you probably need to avoid technical questions about a new system such as:

- How is the proposed financial system upgrade going to interact with the existing personnel system?

- What new modules are going to share data?

Conversely, asking an operational employee, such as a database administrator, questions such as the following is not a good idea either:

- What's your current go-to-market strategy and where do you see your next customer base coming from?

Not that a CEO or a database administrator (DBA) couldn't answer, it's just they aren't the authority and probably don't have full visibility in those areas.

## SCENARIO: ASKING WHY MATTERS

On one occasion I was in a business meeting and listening to a conversation where various managers were discussing the scope of the business problem and trying to map out a strategy and process to address it. Some of the process involved IT. Fred, a junior BA, had been asked to model the problem domain and was presenting it to the managers when Jane asked, somewhat irately:

'You've spent half an hour explaining your notation and how it can model the IT really well and answers the what, when, who and how questions. What we really need to see is "why". So how do you model the "why"?'

Jane was referring to the business strategy and goals. She had been expecting a strategy analysis.

Fred responded: 'Why isn't important, it's just a Post-it Note on a unified modelling language (UML) class diagram.'

Why did Fred say this? Fred looked bemused and moved on to his next point. Obviously Jane didn't know about software. Jane stopped listening and wondered how much more time she'd be wasting today. The UML classes Fred was presenting were part of the design of a software solution and had nothing to do with identifying the business problem. Jane did not invite Fred to further meetings.

The lesson Fred needed to learn is that asking why is important. You might not get answers but at least you asked. Asking why is a good tactic for any level of stakeholder you interview.

Table 2.1 gives you some pointers on questions you might ask to people in different roles. It's important to note again that your context will dictate the specific nature of the questions you ask. The following table simply lists a few questions to present the ideas in this section.

**Table 2.1** Role, question, response

| Role | Your Question | Their Response Might Be |
|---|---|---|
| C-level executive | Why do you need new direction? | Because we are losing market share/product not selling/want to rebrand. |
| | Who is responsible for the new direction? | That's the CIO. It's the IT that's going to get the strategy to work. |
| | Where across the company will there be an impact? | All divisions and primarily marketing, IT, sales, suppliers and customers. |
| | When will the new direction need to be completed? | For example, three years from now. |
| | What steps have been taken to manage the change? | None – big problem. That's why you're here. Find out the big process issues and fix them. |
| | How are you going to measure success? | Stabilisation of customer numbers over next two to three years, looking to an upturn of 20 per cent in the following five. |
| Division manager/general manager/portfolio/ programme manager | What is your division/ department responsible for? | My division has to meet x, y, z strategy. |
| | Who is you main customer or set of customers? | The IT department; the customer. |
| | How are you measuring the success of your actions to meet the strategy? | We collect data on the efficiency of our supply chain. |
| Enterprise architect | Where do you map the business architecture to the technical? | Along these manufacturing processes. |
| | What performance measures are in place? | Throughput is key and we measure it like this. |
| | How does the technical infrastructure support the agility strategy? | That's a really good question; we have improved performance by looking at bottlenecks in the process and in the workflow. |
| Project manager | What is the release date for this product cycle? | Next quarter: 1 September it goes live so we will release on 30 August and give ourselves a day to tidy up. |
| | How are the risks managed over the project lifetime? | I don't think they are. Mostly the risks are in the business case as to be determined (TBDs). |
| Business analyst | Who are the main stakeholders? | Our real stakeholder is any person who needs to renew an existing passport or apply first time. The rest work here. |

| Role | Your Question | Their Response Might Be |
|---|---|---|
| | How do you facilitate communication between business and IT? | I try to liaise as much as possible and also hold twice monthly meetings with business and IT stakeholders. They won't talk to each other and only communicate through me, which is a big problem as it slows down production enormously. We use an anonymous project blog as well. |
| IT designer/developer | Why is this architecture the right one? | We just believe it is. |
| Customer | Where do you feel service could be improved? | Feedback when it all goes wrong – no one tells us anything. We've queued at this airport for three days and no one has said anything to help. |
| User: back office | What is communication like with the front line staff? | We aren't allowed to talk to them directly. We have to use the liaison and that stinks. |
| User: front line staff | What's the most common complaint from customers? | No feedback when something unusual or unexplained happens. |
| Service desk staff | How do you collate customer queries? | From our front line staff – we just put all the queries into one long list in a spreadsheet. |
| | Who do you communicate the query to? | Someone in IT. We just email it to help@IT. |
| QA managers | What's the regression testing strategy for the quarterly release cycle? | We test the new pieces of functionality and the pieces of code those new pieces integrate with directly. |

## ARE YOU GOING TO ASK THE SAME QUESTION TO DIFFERENT INTERVIEWEES?

You might have worked out by now that different roles in an engagement will have different tasks, work at different levels in the company, have different knowledge bases and different responsibilities. This implies rightly that you should ask different questions – this idea is exemplified in Table 2.1. If you do ask the same question to five different roles, the risk you run is that you will get five views on five entirely different topics because each interviewee will interpret what you are asking for differently. What you are aiming to do is get five views of the same thing. You would then identify similarities between what interviewees say – this is discussed further in Chapter 4 on analysis.

But how do you get five views on the same topic? If you're interviewing five project managers about their preferred scheduling approach, then this is easily achieved. But if you're trying to get a coherent picture of a large project and your interviewees range from C-level executives to IT developers and customers, then this is going to be somewhat more difficult. As an example, if you want to find out the impact of technology in supporting a business strategy of increasing market share by 25 per cent by successfully selling a range of new products, you would probably need to word the question differently for different roles. An example of this is shown in Table 2.2.

**Table 2.2    Getting viewpoints**

| Role | Question | Possible Responses |
|------|----------|--------------------|
| Chief information officer | How is IT supporting the increase market share business strategy? | Pretty well aligned, we've just implemented a new sales management system for sales staff to support their operations. This is now fully integrated into the inventory management system in the warehouse and the Customer Relationship Management (CRM) the help support desk people are using. |
| Sales manager | How well does the new sales management system support and report on your drive to attract new customers and get more sales of new products? | The new system is really great for reporting. We can now keep track of the number of product sales and can keep the warehouse up to date on anticipating stock level requirements. So we can count the number of new customers easily and they've gone up by 12 per cent for this quarter compared to this time last year. |
| Customer help desk operator | Has the new CRM system you're using helped you in doing your job in solving customer problems or dealing with their complaints? | No, I find it takes too long to find a customer record and it doesn't show any of their purchase details. So when a customer rings in to complain that their product is faulty or they are having difficulties in setting it up or a part is missing, I really want to see what they ordered in case the warehouse team have put any notes already about product defects and fixes I can quickly recommend. The old paper system worked like that – you just had to go through the pile to get to the right one and match it with the sales record on the old sales system. |

| Role | Question | Possible Responses |
|------|----------|--------------------|
| Warehouse manager | Does the inventory management system get updated automatically now that the sales and CRM systems are integrated with it? | It works brilliantly except that the updates come in as soon as a product has been purchased. The problem with this is that the system automatically sends the supplier a purchase order for the next product. What if we don't want to use that supplier any more or they've gone out of business or they don't stock that product anymore? We used to keep all requests for new products and send them in a weekly batch once we had talked to our suppliers on the phone. It might seem old fashioned but that call made all the difference as the supplier could tell us what was working for them, what they anticipated as coming in next from the manufacturer. Now we've lost that human touch and sometimes our purchase orders are unanswered and more often than not, a supplier will get fed up with the continual orders and call us up moaning why we can't send a batch once a week like we used to. All the supplier does now is collect all the orders and at the end of the week bundle them off as one order to the manufacturer anyway. Trouble is with all those individual orders, the supplier can lose some of the paperwork and we come up short on products – it happens all the time. This is really bad when the demand is high. |
| Customer representative | When you buy a new product have you noticed any change in the service you get? | I can use more credit cards now as I can order online if I want. That's pretty good and the website is really informative and easy to use. The help desk isn't that helpful – they can't ever track down my last order if I have a problem or question about it. That seems to be happening more and more and it is really frustrating. |

As you can see from the examples in Table 2.2, the questions don't ask about strategy except to the CIO, who is knowledgeable about the strategy and the steps to align the IT to support and help deliver upon that. The other interviewees get asked questions that are of direct relevance to them. As an interviewer, you need to plan this story by working out what to ask in advance and then piece the responses together to give a broad and multi-perspective view of what is the same question. A customer is interested in good service and good products at competitive prices. There's no point asking her about the organisation's strategic alignment. All you can glean is that they like the ability to buy products online and this should bring her back to buy more. The help desk is a problem for her though. Saying that, if you consider this view in light of what the sales manager had to say – sales are up by 12 per cent this quarter compared to last year – you might reasonably surmise that growth is happening and the strategy is working and being supported by the IT. Then if you take into account the problems with the help desk and at the warehouse, you might surmise these are areas where improvements and fixes need to be made and the overall effect could boost sales further.

## WHO DO YOU CHOOSE TO FOLLOW UP WITH?

The first answer that comes to mind is everyone you interviewed. This is a reasonable strategy if you only interviewed five or six people. If you interviewed 20 or so people, you might need to think this through a bit more. The real question here isn't whom you need to follow up with but what are the criteria for following up with someone. In other words, you need an upfront list of criteria that if met would merit a follow up. Table 2.3 presents a list I use, with comments.

You can see from the table that I am not advising you follow up and present feedback to all interviewees. In many cases, you won't need to do this, nor will you have time. Be selective about whom you get back to. Some interviewees will want to see some result from the process. Here they are referring to the final report and whether it is acted upon. In this case, you may have to toe the party line: 'I have been asked to produce the report for so-and-so only, I assume you will get a copy from them.'

You must not distribute your final report to all interviewees and interested parties unless you have explicit permission from your client/customer to do so. If you do have such permission, I strongly urge you to tone down the report by making all quotes and comments anonymous. You never know where the report will end up, and once it is delivered your client owns it so she can do what she likes with it at that point, assuming there are no contractual agreements about keeping the report confidential.

Table 2.3    Follow up criteria

| Criteria | Comment | Follow up? Y/N |
|---|---|---|
| Answer to key question(s) unclear | An interviewee might answer the question she thought you wanted answering, not the one you wanted answering. Or the answer was genuinely unclear. | Yes, by email. |
| You ran out of time so didn't ask everything | The interviewee was late or the fire alarm went off or there was a long answer to some questions.<br>If this happened in every interview you are asking too many questions and have not prepared sufficiently. | Yes, if this happens only occasionally. Email or if possible a quick meeting. No, if this happens all the time – review your questions instead. |
| The interviewee is very keen to continue the conversation | The subject of your engagement might be the interviewee's pet hobby. Or the interviewee is really vital to the outcome of your engagement. | Yes, if vital to engagement. No, probably, if the interviewee's hobby but interviewee is not in a key position in the project. |
| You want to validate everything an interviewee said | Some interviewees are more valuable to your project than others. In this case, remember a summary is gold, an unabridged transcript is bad news.<br>Some interviewees are more available and can respond faster than others. The more senior management the interviewee, the less available and slower to respond you should expect them to be.<br>You normally only get one shot at executives so get it right first time. | Yes, if interviewee key and you are uncertain on some of the statements made or really feel uncomfortable using comments unless signed off. A meeting might work better than an email but it depends on availability. |
| You want to validate key points made by any number of interviewees and quote them in the final report | Part of your job might be to present comments made by interviewees either anonymously or openly – you will need to get permission to do so from both the client and the interviewee. | Yes, absolutely. Email is fine. |
| Interviewee requests a summary of interview prior to giving you permission to use it | Some interviewees want to make sure you have represented their viewpoint exactly and will ask for it. If you feel an interviewee is particularly nervous or concerned about feedback, show the interviewee what pieces of the interview you are planning to use in the report. | Yes, provide a one-page summary (assuming the interviewee isn't a 'worry guts' and has little value to the project). Email it. |

## WHAT PROMISES CAN YOU MAKE TO AN INTERVIEWEE?

Some interviewees will be concerned about confidentiality, inference (although the name was removed everyone knows who the person is), the final report and its impact. It is advisable to tell all interviewees prior to the interview that everything said during the interview is confidential and will remain so unless otherwise agreed between all parties. If you're recording the interview, explain that the recording is for your own benefit and no one else's: you need it to cross check your notes, will store it in a safe place and will not pass it on except perhaps to members of your team if it is that person who will do the analysis. The same goes for note taking. This is an important point.

Interviewees may want to appear invisible in the report. However, it is not easy to mask someone if the comments are strong, extremely one-sided or the role that person takes in the company is few and far between: the viewpoint will make it clear who the individual is. You may have to 'blanderise' the report far more than you had anticipated, such as removing role names. Remember, though, that your job is to find things out and make recommendations for courses of action. If you dumb down the juicy parts of the report or mask the interviewee completely, this may have a detrimental effect on your report. You want to have impact with your client but not inadvertently put someone's head on the block, including yours. It is a balance you will have to work out based on context. Five things to consider in this regard are:

1.  Damage factor. Will this comment hurt someone's reputation or put their job at risk if you leave it in?

2.  Report visibility. Who is going to read this report? Is it for public consumption or entirely in-house?

3.  Sensitivity of engagement. Are you uncovering the reasons for an embarrassing and costly project failure? You may have to remove all reference to names and potentially roles in this case.

4.  Client's opinion. Your client will give you an overall feel for how open you can be in reporting. Listen carefully.

5.  Your integrity. You are a professional, irrespective of whether you are a consultant, work in-house or are a researcher. As such, you need to make value judgements about the wishes of interviewees. Most will be unwilling to be named. You should respect their wishes

even if your client finds this unnecessary. Remember, you are dealing with real people.

If you promise to obscure references to individuals, make sure you do so, to the best of your ability. Take into consideration all of the above points but I would err on the side of integrity because if you damage your own reputation, you will struggle to get another engagement.

Interviewees might ask to see a copy of the final report. As I mentioned in the section above, if you are a consultant, the owner of that report is your client. Only upon the express permission of the client should you pass the report to interviewees.

Many interviewees will have opinions about how to fix damage, resolve issues, and deliver better products. They will view the report as a means to an end: 'Tell them everything I say and everything will get fixed.' It doesn't work like that, unfortunately. You might be asked to recommend courses of action. Every interviewee will have an opinion on that and some will be made in ignorance of wider issues or the bigger picture. Your job is to come up with the recommendations that best suit the needs of your client. So don't make any promises.

## MODIFYING THE PLAN AS YOU LEARN MORE

As you learn more about the problem/issues/opportunities from your stakeholders and interviewees, it is always wise to revisit your plan and make amendments as and when appropriate. Things that are highly likely to change are who to interview, interviewee priority and needs, and the questions you ask; as you learn more you will continually sharpen and tailor your questions more appropriately.

Remember to keep the overriding objective for the engagement in mind to ensure you are still aligned and on target. If it is the overriding objective that changes, then your plan will have to change in line with the strategic change. If the scope is changed significantly then think about requesting some more time and reconsider your fee.

## DEVIATING DRAMATICALLY FROM THE PLAN

It is inevitable that at least one interview will deviate to some extent from the plan. There are a number of reasons for this and often it's because of the character of the interviewee combined with the character of the interviewer that allow interviews to fall off course as soon as they start. Note that I am not going to present a psychological profile of each. There are far more qualified experts out there for that. If you are interested in personality types a good place to start is a book by David Keirsey where he expands on personality types as identified by a Myers-Briggs assessment.[1]

Chapter 3 discusses further about how to pull interviews, and interviewees, back on course should the interview go off the rails. But before we get to that point, let's take a look at the case study we will be following for the rest of the book.

## Case Study: Potato Grow Ltd Strategic Initiative

We will be following a case study in order to highlight the flexibility and range of the analysis and modelling tools described in this book. 'Potato Grow Ltd' describes a strategic initiative to modernise practices and technology in order to increase business for a goods supplier.

### CONTEXT

A medium-sized organisation, Potato Grow Ltd, manages the supply of potatoes to a leading producer of frozen potato products such as oven chips. Potato Grow decided to expand its footprint into the potato patch to become a major player in the potato supply sector. Potato Grow takes its impact on the environment very seriously and only works with organic farms that do not use pesticides of any kind or genetically modified organisms (GMO), both of which cause cancer and are designed to kill life. A critical goal for Potato Grow is to make sure its farming practices remain ethical and organic, with a longer-term goal of reducing its carbon footprint to zero.

Table 2.4 presents a completed global checklist by Karl Land Ltd's lead consultant in preparation for the engagement with Potato Grow.

1   David Keirsey, *Please Understand Me II: Temperament, Character, Intelligence*, Del Mar, CA, Prometheus Nemesis Book Company; 1st edition 1998.

**Table 2.4  Global checklist for Potato Grow Ltd**

| # | Item | Answer? | Responsible and Contact | Issues |
|---|------|---------|-------------------------|--------|
| I | What is the overriding objective for the engagement? | To independently validate the strategic initiative that Potato Grow has conceived, to identify and highlight any inconsistencies there might be and make recommendations for improvements. | karlC@KL BobH@PG, (CEO) | None – timing suits us as much as PG. |
| 2 | What is the context of the engagement? | Potato Grow wants to expand its UK-based and European business and has begun a new strategic initiative to do this. PG is a medium-sized player loyal to its organic farmers. Recognised in sector for superior product (fresh potato) but appears to be facing stiffer competition. Some bad press around losing major customer within the last year. See attachment for further details and references. | karlC@KL BobH@PG | None – time frame short but can be done if work commences in two weeks (date). |
| 3 | Who are you going to interview? | See list attached – range looks to be from executives to operations in PG plus a selection of farmers. Missing logistics partners? | KarlC, BobH@PG's administrator: admin@PG | Will have to ensure enough coverage as numbers look to be around 12–15. |
| 4 | Who are the high-priority interviewees? | TBD. | — | BH may have an opinion on this – will need to ask. |
| 5 | In what order should you interview people? | See attached list. | BobH@PG's administrator: admin@PG | Would like to interview management at PG before operations to get big picture first. |
| 6 | When should the interview happen? | See attached schedule. | BobH@PG's administrator: admin@PG | Looks OK though six interviews per day may be too much. Will push for four a day max. |

**Table 2.4**     *continued*

| # | Item | Answer? | Responsible and Contact | Issues |
|---|------|---------|-------------------------|--------|
| 7 | Where should the interview take place? | Have set up an office at PG HQ though will have to travel to farms. | BobH@PG's administrator: admin@PG | Will have to check in advance that farms have a quiet room for interview. Distances to–from farms from HQ vary – may delay delivery of report by up to one week. Will need to check with BobH this is acceptable. |
| 8 | What equipment should you take into an interview? | Usual (pens, notebook, iPod). | KarlC | Make sure iPod charged with cable. |
| 9 | Who arranges the interviews? | Done. BobH's admin at PG. | BobH's admin at PG | Check with interviewees in advance they know their schedule. |
| 10 | What is an optimal number of interviews for your engagement? | 12–15 selected in advance; anticipate five or so more. | KarlC | Will need approval from BobH if extra interviews start to take up too much time? |
| 11 | How long do you have to do the interviews? | One week scheduled but this is for interviews themselves. Will need two extra weeks to conduct analysis. | KarlC, BobH | Will need to ask for leeway if analysis gets particularly complex (for example, one extra week). |
| 12 | Will there by follow ups/ feedback? | Yes (feedback not planned unless requested). | KarlC, BobH | Follow up will be OK but feedback to individual interviewees needs clearance from BobH. |
| 13 | How many interviewers do you need? | Two in total – check Heinz is available. | KarlC | If Heinz unavailable for all, then check if June can sit in when Heinz can't be there. |
| 14 | Are there special instructions from your client about the interview plan or subsequent phases? | None thus far – no impression there will be. | KarlC, BobH | None. |

Table 2.4 provides limited detail about the main global issues around the engagement as well as arranging the interviews. There are several references to lists and documents that would have been collated as part of the project's early documentation. You would want much more information about the context of the engagement than would reasonably fit into the table. Also, the list of interviewees may be long so may not reasonably fit. Remember the checklist is a pointer or reminder to you to make sure you have organised and planned enough for you to commence the engagement effectively. Once you have the global list in place, this holds for all interviews and activities on the project. You'll need to then start planning for each interview. Table 2.5 presents an 'interview specific' list for an interview at Potato Grow.

Note that the specific list items have been slightly reworded to refer to 'this' interview rather than the more generic 'each' interview as described in Table 2.4 above.

Table 2.5    Interview specific list example, Potato Grow Ltd

| Interviewee: Joe, Initiative Lead, Supply Chain and Customer Relations Director<br>Location: PG HQ Room L17<br>Time: 11.30am<br>Date: Tues 22 March 2015 | Interviewers: Karl and Heinz |
|---|---|
| **# Item** | **Answers?** |
| 1   What are the key objectives for this interview? | 1. Identify key strategies and Vision for initiative.<br>2. Identify structure of supply chain and proposed changes.<br>3. Understand the potential conflicts in initiative against environmental policy. |
| 2   What is the specific context for this interview? | Second interview in engagement and need to know about the bigger picture of the initiative, of Potato Grow's business and current processes to realise the potential impact of the proposed initiative and its desire to be a leading zero carbon footprint and recognised environmentally friendly organisation. |
| 3   What key questions are you going to ask? | 1. Tell me about your business and roles. (Help understand interview Objectives 1, 2 and 3).<br>2. Can you describe the current supply line structure and how you would change it?<br>3. What's the overall objective of the proposed strategic initiative? (Interview Objective 1).<br>4. Tell me about your new environmental policy. (Objectives 1 and 3).<br>5. How has it changed? (Objectives 1 and 3).<br>6. Where do you foresee conflict between the strategic initiative and the environmental policy? (Objective 3). |

**Table 2.5** *continued*

| # | Item | Answers? |
|---|------|----------|
| 4 | Follow up with interviewee? | Definitely, given role of strategic initiative lead. |
| 5 | What promises can you make to an interviewee? | TBD – depends on CEO. |
| 6 | Modifying the plan as you learn more | Second interview in engagement so unlikely to change much now. |

The first thing you might note in Table 2.5 is that there are only six questions listed. It would be unlikely for you list all the questions that will be asked primarily because a number may only occur to you during the course of the interview itself. However, the questions listed in point (3) are key ones in that they directly refer to the objectives for the interview itself. The context (point 2) sets the scene and shows this is the second interview in the engagement. The last three points would only become relevant later into the engagement, though given the importance of this role it would be wise to follow up with Joe when needed.

## Summary

This chapter has given you an interview specific list that you can use to help you prepare before each interview.

Remember this is a chapter about *planning* the interview question. Once you've completed the question plan that you feel comfortable with or at least able to commence with, you have to be able to conduct the interviews and that involves a whole set of different skills and organisation. This is discussed next.

# Chapter 3

# Conducting the Interview: What to Say

People who like to talk should be great interviewers, shouldn't they? Well, not always. There is a lot of skill needed to keep an interview in tow and on track. It's really easy to lose control of the subject and the time. This often happens because interviews make people nervous. Interviewees can be really worried about interviews: why am I being interrogated? Will what I say come back to haunt me? Why am I being singled out? Will what I say make any difference anyway? Interviewers can also get nervous, particularly if the interviews aren't going to plan … remember my former colleague in the preface to this book?

This chapter gives you an overview of how to manage an interview in terms of keeping it on track and on time by the things you say, when you say them and *how* you say them. Here are two absolutely true stories that illustrate how easy it is to run off track and not get what you want.

## SCENARIOS: TOO MUCH TALKING IN INTERVIEWS

1. I once worked with a colleague who loved to talk. He loved talking and listening – in short he was a good conversationalist. We had a market research project to fulfil and he conducted a number of interviews with high-ranking staff in a number of companies. Because he loved to converse and he loved to explore different avenues, we would always get really fascinating interview transcripts. But we didn't get the answers we wanted because he didn't ask the right questions. He didn't ask the questions, although we had planned the interviews quite well, because when an interviewee went off on a tangent, he didn't pull them back in and ultimately lost track of where he should be. He even suggested different tangents himself, sometimes pushing the interviewee down paths that were not relevant to the engagement's overriding objective. The result was we simply didn't get anywhere near

enough information to do a good job and as a result our analysis was found wanting.

2.      I was once interviewed for a job at a global company and though I conducted myself pretty well – or so I thought until I wasn't offered the post – the two interviewers were obviously unprepared and were taking the opportunity to skip an extra hour or so off work. They talked and talked, ad-libbing, asking all kinds of irrelevant questions in an exceedingly random manner. I think by the time the two-hour-plus interview was over, we were all sick of the sight of each other. The interviewers didn't know when to wrap up the interview, nor how to keep it flowing on course, at pace and with ease.

Chapters 1 and 2 provided guidelines on how to plan an effective and efficient interview. This chapter walks you through how to put that plan into action.

## The Interview Lifecycle

Most interviews, if conducted appropriately, go through a set number of phases that for all intents and purposes can be labelled the interview lifecycle:

- Warm Up

- Setting the Direction

- Main Event

- Wrap Up

- Warm Down.

We will look at each of these one by one; in the 'main event' section we will walk through an interview from the strategic initiative case, Potato Grow.

## Warm Up

As I said at the start of this chapter, both interviewees *and* interviewers can be a bit nervous. It's particularly the case with the interviewee when your brief is to find out what went wrong on a recent project. Putting interviewees at ease as soon as possible ensures you'll get the most out of them. So why not start with some ice breaking chatter?

If you're conducting a post mortem review, tell the interviewee this is not a witch hunt – they won't believe you but you should try nonetheless.

Tell the interviewee the purpose of the interview is to ascertain what happened – in a post mortem review – both good and bad, and to figure out how to make it all good next time, that you are not looking for scapegoats. Tell the interviewee this is an opportunity to say what she thinks happened, and to suggest how it can be fixed/improved for next time round. Talk small talk – it's an art. I am hopeless at it in general but I am good at putting interviewees at ease, or as much at ease as possible when the interviewee first enters the interview room, settles into a chair and surveys their surroundings. You have to learn small talk. I normally introduce myself, giving the interviewee some background on who I am. Just be careful this does not become the main topic of the interview.

Don't sit there silently brooding like a courtroom judge about to condemn a poor soul. Stand up when the interviewee comes into the room. If the interviewee is waiting outside, go meet him and invite him in. Smile. Shake hands.

## ICE BREAKERS STYLE POINTERS

*Good Style*: 'Hi, I'm Karl. (Shake hands) Is this a good time for you to meet? Tell me about what you do.' Refer to their job role – people love to talk about themselves, even the shy ones – you can elaborate a bit, follow the conversation if it's in line with the interview objectives.

The warm up should only last three or so minutes. You don't have much time to waste but you also cannot afford to miss the warm up.

There's one more thing you need to do before setting the direction and that's turning your recording device on. Don't start recording the minute the interviewee is in his chair because you'll waste your batteries skipping through the warm up chatter. Make sure the recording device has been visible on the desk in front of the interviewee since entering the room. This will weaken the interviewee's resolve to refuse the recording by making the recording device less alien an object by the time you get to this point. You should say:

'Do you mind if I record this interview? I will only use the recordings to check my notes and no one else shall hear it. I shall then erase it.'

Most interviewees are quite happy to be recorded. Turn it on quickly and position the device slightly closer to the interviewee than yourself but not right under his nose. If the interviewee is worried about being recorded, don't ignore this. It's better to not switch the device on. This is when a thick notepad comes in handy, and a scribe!

## Setting the Direction

You only have at most 60 minutes for the entire interview. In reality this is 50 minutes because it takes time to settle. Also, interviewees prefer to get to their next appointment/activity on schedule. As an interviewer you will need a break as well. So you need to get going as fast as to think the ice is cracking. That means you need to rapidly set up the direction for the interview. Ask the question, 'What were you told about the purpose of the interview?' More often than not I have got a reply along the lines of, 'I don't really know. All I got was an email saying there was a review going on of the new process/ tool/application being planned and I was going to be interviewed. It didn't say anything about you and I didn't know there was a review/new project underway' or 'I have not been told the purpose of the review other than it is happening.'Quite often in an internal review interviewees will be volunteered involuntarily and will not have been given enough background as to what the review objectives really are, so will have formed their own, mostly negative, opinions. They will need to be reassured as to why they have been chosen for the interview and what you are really trying to achieve. Tell them the truth quickly and succinctly. If you can't tell the truth because your client wants you to say something else, find another client. Once you have set the scene, you need to drive the interview in that direction. Your first and most important question so far is going to be:

- 'Tell me about your job/role/involvement in the project/proposed system/process/business unit' and so on, or put another way;

- 'Tell me about your business and what you do'; or

- 'Tell me what you are planning to do and why.'

The trick is to get as much useful information as possible and avoid all the other flannel you will no doubt hear. You will need to cut off the interviewee to get into the main body of the interview. If you don't you'll find the interviewee will either:

- tell you the story of his life;

- tell you what's wrong with the world entire;

- not say enough.

You will find some interviewees will give you the one-second elevator pitch:

- 'I'm the DBA.'

If this happens, you will have to tease some more information out of the interviewee:

- 'So what do you do in your job as a DBA?'

… answer …

- 'Oh, really? So who do you work with to do that?'

… answer …

- 'Ah, so you're responsible for "x" and so-and-so is meant to give you all the data about "y"? How is that data transferred? How do you respond to emergencies when a customer's database crashes or a bug creeps into it at 2 a.m.?'

… answer …

… and so on. You play question and answer tag in these circumstances until you get enough to move on to the main body of the interview. The key is to ask only useful questions. This means you have to think a little about what to ask and follow the conversation to the point where you believe the interviewee is finally at ease and primed for the main event. At this point, you can get on with the key questions. I wouldn't spend more than five minutes on the direction setting. Most interviewees will pick up the direction and purpose of the interview really quickly, in a lot less time than you think. Those that truly do not get it are probably the wrong people to interview in the first place. But you'll really only know this once you get to the main part of the interview.

## A COMMENT ON QUESTION STYLES

### Open-ended questions

Some people suggest that the best way to elicit the juiciest nuggets of information from a customer or supplier or whoever you are interviewing is to use entirely open-ended questions. The concern I have for the open-ended approach is that people misunderstand what open-ended actually means. As an example, a colleague, when advising a student on an industrial project, might suggest he didn't agree with the approach to interviewing described in this book, because there was a risk the student would miss something critical if she just kept only to her prescribed questions. This colleague recommended to have no planned questions at all. He misunderstood what open questions mean in interviews. Having not planned any questions at all is not the same as having planned a number of open questions to ask. My response to this scenario is: no planned questions will only lead to a doomed interview. I do not advocate sticking to your questions whatever the situation or direction the interview takes. I recommend a degree of agility but agility built upon firm foundations: having conducted all of the necessary planning activities described in Chapters 1 and 2 that fit your context.

If you have no planned questions, either written down or in your head and/or no overriding objective and/or you have no contextual understanding of the business/engagement, then you are going to end up in a lot of trouble. You won't know what to ask if you have no planned questions. You won't know if you're asking the right questions if you have little to no contextual knowledge. You won't know if you've achieved what you set out to achieve if you don't know the objective for the engagement or the specific objectives and context of each interview. How can you manage your schedule if you've no idea what to ask? How can you select the right people to interview if you have no idea what the context of the engagement is? How can you pitch your questions at the right level if you haven't planned at least some of them in advance?

There are some advantages with asking open questions. You can follow a train of thought if you think it relevant and the interviewee agrees. The interviewee might even say, 'That's a very good question' and continue the train of thought. The danger is that you will follow too far and not be able to pull yourself and the interview back on course. You have to be direct when pulling back someone in full flow: 'That's really interesting. Can I ask you this? ... (ask question)'.

The interviewee might do double take there and then or might comment on the sudden change in direction, but mostly he will think for a bit and then answer your question.

## Closed questions

Closed questions elicit 'yes/no' or quite short responses. These are useful in interviews as lead-ins to more open, discursive or exploratory questions. I use them as hooks. An example closed question hook:

- Me: 'Have you been affected by the new virus in the printer driver?'

- Interviewee: 'Yes.'

- Me: 'Oh, how were you affected and what was the impact of that?'

- Interviewee: 'Well, it was a disaster because ... '

See how easy it is? The danger of only using closed questions is that you never get to the heart of an issue because you only ever get yes/no responses. You don't get any context or subjectivity or perspective which provides the richness you need to understand the real problem/opportunity and present you with a picture of how to address that problem/opportunity.

My advice is to plan the questions you want to ask. Some will be closed and are necessary as lead-ins to the open questions. Follow trains of thought to get those 'nuggets' you had simply not known about so had not considered. But be prepared to pull the interview back on course to get to any key questions you planned to ask that are still key to your interview.

## Main Event

The way you manage the main body of the interview is going to be fundamentally different dependent upon the context of the engagement. If you are conducting a post mortem review of a disastrous project and are holding interviews to find out what the systemic causes of failure were, then there will be certain questions and a specific process you can use as a guide for finding out key information in that project. If you are working on a strategic initiative and it's your job to work out how to ensure a process or technology innovation is actually going to support that strategic direction, there's a specific approach you can use as a guide for that.

## THE STRATEGIC INITIATIVE INTERVIEW APPROACH

A strategic initiative can be many things and to try and understand all of them in one go is overwhelming. In our case, I am going to break down elements of an initiative into two very simple concepts of what we want to achieve (goals) and who will achieve it (context).[1]

### Goals

Goals, strategies and tactics are things that people want to achieve, and want the business to achieve or do. These can be strategies, objectives, Vision statements, tasks or processes. A goal is typically an 'end-state' which is essentially a condition we want our business or part of it, such as process, to be in. Examples might be that in 2019 our company will have increased its customer base by 20 per cent from our current 2016 customer numbers. This is a hard goal in that there is a direct way to measure its achievement: count the number of customers that we have now and work out how many more will equate to a 20 per cent increase. The goal gives no indication of how we might achieve that target. Hard goals tend to support softer goals. A soft goal is one that is not directly measurable but is only assessed as a result of being able to measure outcomes of its supporting hard goals. An obvious example of a soft goal is a company's Vision statement. This might be something along the lines of: 'To continually strive to enrich the lives of our customers.' How would you imagine achieving this? A mission statement might be the first step and this is in effect a soft strategy. A mission statement in this case might be: 'To provide our customers with the products they want and need when they want and need them.' All we know for sure is that to achieve the Vision we need to provide products of quality or at least to a level that customers want and need them, and to deliver them at the right moment in time when customers realise they need the products. Concrete strategies normally help achieve the mission. Strategies and tactics are doing things that explain how those goals can be achieved or more often than not how we help achieve the goals. A strategy for achieving our example goal might be to promote a new marketing campaign

---

1   These concepts have evolved from ideas originally published in, for example, Steven Bleistein, Karl Cox and June Verner (2006), 'Validating Strategic Alignment of Organisational IT Requirements using Goal Modeling and Problem Diagrams', *Journal of Systems and Software*, 79 (3), pp. 362–78.

over the next four years. A tactic or set of tactics will support the strategy. An example tactic might be to widen the marketing campaign from traditional media of newspapers and television to also promote through new media of digital marketing.

## Context

Business partners such as companies, departments, products, IT systems and individuals work together to deliver the goals. A partner is in fact a role. As an example, a company may have several customer service representatives who all do the same job. So there is a role called customer service representative whose tasks can be performed by many different individuals. The same concept holds for customer. You hope to have more than one customer. You may also have more than one database. You may have multiple business partners in a supply chain that are necessary to help deliver value to a set of customers. Those business partners may be your direct customer, which is different to the end consumer or customer purchasing the final product. It depends where you fit in the supply chain. Some partners are entirely responsible for achieving goals and implementing strategies and tactics to achieve those goals. These could be departments. For example, the marketing department may be solely responsible for the strategy to widen the media through which the company advertises. The IT and marketing departments might be equally responsible for the tactic of moving to the medium of digital marketing.

These straightforward concepts can get at the heart of a business strategy initiative and are discussed in much more detail in Chapter 4 on analysis. These concepts are also very useful in producing diagrams or pictures, or more technically, models, as explained in Chapter 5. The flowchart in Figure 3.1 gives you a simple framework for producing such a graphical model. This is elaborated upon in Chapter 4 and 5. For now, we are interested in asking the right questions and getting the right answers.

The flowchart in Figure 3.1 and the subsequent section will help you to:

- capture much of the information you need to build a picture of the initiative;

- keep the interview within the time frame of one hour;

- speed up analysis and form the basis for the models you may wish to produce, if you need them.

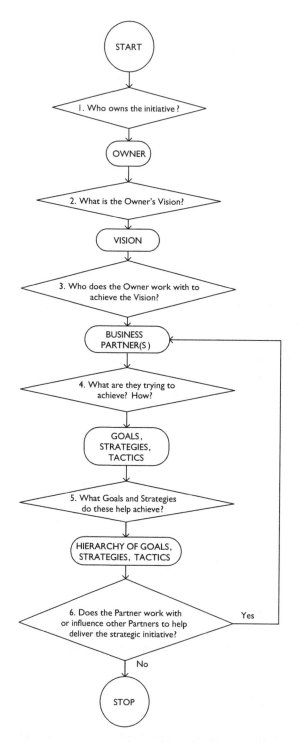

**Figure 3.1    Flow diagram of interview question structure**

Take a look at Figure 3.1. You will see a rigid structure that seems to be dictating what you do in an interview to find out only a few specific things, such as goals, partners and something called a goal hierarchy. The first point for you to note is that you will rarely follow this flowchart verbatim. Then why put it in the book? The reasons are:

1.      I could have presented a table of things to ask about but you wouldn't know what one meant in terms of the other. The flowchart gives you a different perspective.

2.      The flowchart presents you with a structure to ask far more questions than you can see in Figure 3.1 *and know* that you have not missed anything.

The best way to explain is through example. So here's an interview snippet that makes use of the flowchart. Can you spot when the interviewer makes reference to the flowchart?

## POTATO GROW LTD CASE INTERVIEW

The following will take you through an interview so that you get the idea of how to actually manage one as an interviewer. I start by presenting some background that you will have already established prior to the interview from your background reading and other interviews, and identified objectives for the interview itself. Note I am repeating case material as introduced at the end of Chapter 2.

### Context

A medium-sized organisation, Potato Grow Ltd, manages the supply of potatoes to a leading producer of frozen potato products such as oven chips. Potato Grow decided to expand its footprint into the potato patch to become a major player in the potato supply sector. Potato Grow takes its impact on the environment very seriously and only works with organic farms who do not use pesticides of any kind or GMOs, both of which cause cancer and are designed to kill life. A critical goal for Potato Grow is to make sure its farming practices remain ethical and organic, with a longer-term goal of reducing its carbon footprint to zero.

*Engagement objective*

To independently validate the strategic initiative that Potato Grow has conceived, to identify and highlight any inconsistencies there might be and make recommendations for improvements.

Table 3.1 repeats Table 2.5. The interview we are going to examine is the one conducted with Joe, who plays several roles: strategic initiative lead, supply chain director and customer relations director. Joe is a very senior executive in Potato Grow so we are anticipating gathering some really rich and interesting information about Potato Grow and its new initiative.

**Table 3.1     Table 2.5 revisited: Interview specific list example, Potato Grow Ltd**

| Interviewee: Joe, Initiative Lead, Supply Chain and Customer Relations Director<br>Location: PG HQ Room L17<br>Time: 11.30am<br>Date: Tues 22 March 2015 | Interviewers: Karl and Heinz |
|---|---|
| **# Item** | **Answers?** |
| 1  What are the key objectives for this interview? | 1. Identify key strategies and Vision for initiative.<br>2. Identify structure of supply chain and proposed changes.<br>3. Understand the potential conflicts in initiative against environmental policy. |
| 2  What is the specific context for this interview? | Second interview in engagement and need to know about the bigger picture of the initiative, of Potato Grow's business and current processes to realise the potential impact of the proposed initiative and its desire to be a leading zero carbon footprint and recognised environmentally friendly organisation. |
| 3  What key questions are you going to ask? | 1. Tell me about your business and roles. (Help understand Interview Objectives 1, 2 and 3).<br>2. Can you describe the current supply line structure and how you would change it?<br>3. What's the overall objective of the proposed strategic initiative? (Interview Objective 1).<br>4. Tell me about your new environmental policy. (Objectives 1 and 3).<br>5. How has it changed? (Objectives 1 and 3).<br>6. Where do you foresee conflict between the strategic initiative and the environmental policy? (Objective 3). |

| # | Item | Answers? |
|---|------|----------|
| 4 | Follow up with interviewee? | Definitely, given role of strategic initiative lead. |
| 5 | What promises can you make to an interviewee? | TBD – depends on CEO. |
| 6 | Modifying the plan as you learn more | Second interview in engagement so unlikely to change much now. |

Throughout the interview transcript, I will add comments like this [ … comment … ] to show how Joe's answers will help in the overall engagement objective. I will refer back to the flowchart in Figure 3.1 to show when I have extracted information relevant to the flowchart. This will help in understanding the analysis approach in Chapter 4. Note that I do not follow a prescriptive step-by-step approach with regards to the flowchart. In theory, this will work every time but in practice it is a very good guide. The idea of the flowchart is to help relate elements of what the interviewee says to other elements and for the interviewer to provide a framework for asking questions that will extract information that will be necessary to get a better picture of the initiative.

## The interview transcript

Me: Tell me about your business and your various roles, Joe.

[Comment: Once into the main event there is no messing about. Ask those key questions. The first questions should be about the current context of the role(s) Joe plays in Potato Grow. This is important because it reaffirms your understanding of the business and also provides a structure for understanding where the strategic initiative is starting from as well.]

Joe: OK. Let me start with Potato Grow and then I'll talk about my roles in it. What Potato Grow basically does is source quality, organically grown – that's an important point and a mantra for us – potato crops from around the country to supply them to PFreeze, you know: the world leader in frozen chips and waffles, and other smaller frozen potato goods producers, who also turn our potatoes into frozen oven chips and potato waffles and other frozen goods. We've been doing this for 20 years – that's it in a nutshell.

[Comment: It should be obvious that Potato Grow is our business owner in answer to Question 1 in the flowchart in Figure 3.1. Other roles, such as PFreeze, will be a partner. A key business goal of Potato Grow is to supply quality, organically grown potatoes to PFreeze and other smaller producers, collectively let's just call them 'customers', addressing Question 3 in the flowchart. We will call them customers rather than goods producers because in the context of Potato Grow's business, they are its actual customers.]

Me: OK, so in terms of your roles, I see you play many of them?

Joe: That's true. Normally I am the supply chain director and nothing more. But I am currently acting customer relations director as Bob is off sick for six months – broke both legs and arms and just about everything else in a ski accident – so I get to talk closely with PFreeze and others. I did that anyway because of the supply chain role though from a different perspective. As supply chain lead I liaise with our customers differently and did not consider things like product orders and product quality and how we deal with customers. The supply chain role is more about making sure our logistics people get the right orders to the right customers at the right time. So it's interesting to see a different side of the business. I had no idea how picky our customers are with our potatoes! They are real sticklers for quality. Fortunately we have been in a good position to provide the best quality. On top of that in my spare time [he laughs here and I smile] I'm now running this strategic initiative. It's not a big deal, just ripping apart everything we do and starting again so we can become a big time player in this industry.

[Comment: This is invaluable information for you. You now know a great deal about the management of Potato Grow and it has become clear that Joe is someone you will want to come back to and talk with throughout this engagement.]

Me: That sounds like a real overload of responsibilities, Joe.

Joe: It is.

Me: Can we get back to the business and some of its processes? So when an order comes in from PFreeze, you check availability with the potato farms, right? The farms send you a response of what's in stock and you get back to PFreeze with a Yes/No response?

Joe: About right except we only have a 'Yes' response. We just qualify it with a 'how long it will take' proviso. PFreeze will say 'OK' and the purchase order is raised. We send the order to the farms. They send us a 'yes we can do it to schedule' reply. Our logistics provider helps us fulfil the order as they collect the potatoes and take them to freeze. Our farm invoices us, we invoice PFreeze, they pay us once they have got the delivery and are happy, logistics invoice us too, we pay them and the farm after we have the money from PFreeze, which should be the last working day of each month. In a nutshell.

Me: Is the process the same with other small producers of frozen potato goods?

Joe: Exactly the same.

[Comment: In the above conversation, I take the liberty to walk through the basic supply chain scenario to ascertain that my contextual understanding is correct – in effect asking the first part of Question 2 of the listed interview questions from Table 3.1 above. It may appear that I am being a little bullish in approach. I am. It's important to take the lead as the interviewer because: (1) it allows you to confirm your understanding of your client's basic business and context; (2) it shows the interviewee that you have taken a serious interest in his business and as such he should be more willing to confide in you; and (3) it should give the interviewee a greater feeling of confidence in you. We have rapidly extracted a (very) high-level view of the current business of Potato Grow.]

Me: So tell me about the new initiative.

Joe: We've been stuck in the same market, same product, same suppliers, in a rut, for about five years now. There are few competitors but they've always been there. This last year, we've lost out on a couple of large orders because our potato suppliers have been smaller farms. We have traditionally supported smaller farms. But we couldn't get our act together to source potatoes from a number of those farms at one go to meet the orders. A couple of our competitors have very large suppliers. Their potatoes aren't as high quality as ours and, critically for us, their potatoes are not organically grown, but that didn't seem to matter to the customer: they obviously changed their opinion about environmentally friendly farming methods and organic produce. We have got to find a way to meet the new massive demand for potatoes without damaging our reputation as a provider of organic potatoes. Actually, we've decided to push even further into environmentally friendly production of potatoes with our new Environmental Strategy.

[Comment: Meeting new massive demand is close to the Vision for Potato Grow's initiative.]

Me: Let's come to the Environmental Strategy in a minute …

[Comment: Though the Environmental Strategy is a very important one for Potato Grow, I have deliberately pushed it to one side for now. It's OK to do that because you need to be able to continue your train of thought or line of questions before coming back to that Environmental Strategy.]

Joe: OK.

Me: … and, in a way, my next question might be relevant to that: why don't you just form a cooperative among the farmers that supply you?

Joe: We have but it hasn't been as effective as we wanted. We need to be able to monitor crops and potato availability if we are going to meet those large orders.

[Comment: Here is an important tactic, 'Monitor crops and potato availability to meet large orders'. Who is responsible for its achievement? It looks like Potato Grow has a vested interest and the farms themselves.]

Me: What turnaround time does the client expect on orders?

Joe: About a week from order to potato delivery. Potatoes have a long shelf life but need to be really fresh to keep their flavour and texture when they get turned into oven chips.

Me: What's the average turnaround time now?

Joe: There isn't one. We just can't meet that demand. We are turning away customers who won't accept a smaller delivery in a longer time frame, normally two weeks minimum.

[Comment: Clearly there is a major operational/process problem here: delays in meeting orders are losing customers and that's bad. So I decide to follow this thread a little further and delay getting to that Environmental Strategy.]

Me: How many customers are being disappointed?

Joe: Two, like I said.

Me: Just two?

[Comment: Joe looks apprehensive, thinks for a second, then asks for my iPod to be switched off for what he is about to say; I stop the recording.]

Joe: Well, actually, you didn't hear this from me, but we've lost nine contracts in the last four months. Our margins are small and shrinking and our customers are ordering larger quantities. We've got a steady supply of smaller orders that help keep the lights on but the way things are going we've got 18 to 24 months before we go under if we don't act now.

[Comment: Here's the crux. Potato Grow will potentially go out of business in two years if the situation remains as it is. Hence, we have a pretty serious strategic initiative we need to find out about. Once Joe is feeling more relaxed, I ask him if I can restart the recording. He consents. I switch my iPod back on and move onto the strategic initiative.]

Me: Tell me about the strategic initiative.

Joe: We've decided that we need to bring potato supply in line with demand and to exceed projected demand over the next five years.

Me: This is the project Vision? To bring potato supply up to meet and exceed projected demand over the next five years?

Joe: Absolutely, that's the agreed Vision.

[Comment: You will check with other interviewees what their take on the Vision is.]

Me: Exceed demand? Why 'exceed'?

Joe: We're not sure about the European market. Worst case it remains the same as now for us, which is pretty small but it might take off if we can meet larger demands.

Me: OK, that makes sense. Do you have any estimates on how big that demand will be?

Joe: Yes, we've projected figures for each year with seasonal variations for the next five years based on worst case, average and best-case scenarios.

Me: How far off the mark is current capacity to the best-case scenario?

Joe: About 200 per cent off.

[Comment: Goal: 'Increase potato capacity by 200 per cent'. The next question I'd ask is:]

Me: By when?

Joe: Within the next 12 months.

[Comment: This qualifies the goal and gives you the key performance indicator to assess whether it has been achieved. So I'd add the qualifier to the goal so that it now reads, 'Increase potato capacity by 200 per cent within 12 months'.]

Me: Wait a minute, but don't you have a five-year plan?

Joe: Yes, overall we have the five-year target. But we have some more immediate goals to hit otherwise we are going to struggle to make the five years.

Me: How are you going to do this?

Joe: We need a monitoring system in place to tell us the crop and potato availability to handle large orders.

Me: Ah, so you want to be able to check centrally, and instantaneously, whether you have the potatoes immediately available through some kind of IT system.

Joe: Exactly.

[Comment: Note that this goal, 'To be able to check centrally … ' can only be realised by, 'Monitoring crop and potato availability to meet large orders'. This gives you a sense of goal dependency or hierarchy.]

Me: How are you going to transform the supplier farms and crop size in 12 months?

Joe: We've thought about this and we believe we can manage the physical transformation – provide centralised storage facilities at the farms within 12 months. We think the technology part will take three years to be delivered. That will give us two years to try and reap some major returns.

[Comment: A tactic for Potato Grow and farms is 'provide centralised storage facilities'.]

Me: But what about the crop size? Do you have enough farms on your books?

Joe: No, we need to recruit 100 per cent more farmers and their farms. Or put it another way, we need 100 per cent more potatoes to meet demand. And of course, we can only deal with organic farms and organically grown potatoes. It's PG's mantra.

Me: Somehow I am getting the impression the new Environmental Strategy that I've heard a lot about but don't know what it really is in detail may make your job harder, not easier. Would I be right?

[Comment: Finally back to that Environmental Strategy and Question 4 in our list of questions. Note it is not a word-for-word rendition of the question but it should be good enough to get the response you want.]

Joe: Your impression may be very close to the mark. But let me quote you the Environmental Strategy – which is really a mantra, 'Potato Grow promises the earth that it will in no way harm its soil nor its sky nor anything that lives and breathes between the two.'

Me: OK. Well actually I like that. How are you planning to implement that?

Joe: No idea. But this is what we hope we can do. We hope we can continue our ethical farming practices on our farms, you know, farm in an entirely organic way. We hope by clustering our farms into larger collectives we can take the best environmental farming principles and apply these to the whole cluster. We need to recruit ethical farmers and their farms. We need to look at our packaging and transportation/supply chain processes to reduce our carbon footprint to zero – I've no idea how we hit the 'carbon zero' target, solar-powered lorries?

[Comment: Strategies: 'continue ethical farming practices', 'apply best environmental practices to cluster to bring about efficiencies', 'recruit ethical farmers/farms', 'examine supply chain and transportation to reduce carbon footprint' – to achieve goal 'zero carbon footprint'.]

Me: This seems to be a mix of making sure you farm organically and ethically and also to reduce energy usage so carbon emissions drop. Would that be right?

Joe: That's about right. Right now our farms are monitored by the Soil Association and we are certified as being purely organic. As we expand our business we will need to make sure we are adhering to the Soil Association's targets. We also have this energy reduction target for all our business. One goal appears to be certification of ISO16001 – having an Energy Management System in place or something like that. We are in discussion with the Carbon Trust and they have agreed to provide support, not for free, and monitor our progress in meeting the standard targets. We want to make sure we have everything in place to meet that standard so that we can drive towards that zero carbon footprint.

[Comment: The strategies we just identified relate to two different areas: farming practices and carbon emissions from energy usage. We will need to separate these out: those strategies directly relating to farming will need to support achievement of an ethical farming goal in order to remain organic and maintain certification. Those strategies around reducing energy usage should support achievement of the 'zero carbon footprint' goal. There is a target goal of 'ISO16001 certification' and this seems to be achievable with the help of an Energy Management System. We also have new business partners: Soil Association for certification in organic farming, Carbon Trust in monitoring progress towards ISO16001 certification.]

Me: OK. What's the catch?

Joe: First let me state I am a believer in ethical farming and reducing our energy consumption. But there is a catch and it is two-fold. First, we simply don't have enough ethical farms in the country to meet projected demands. Right now, we partner with nearly 65 per cent of them. So to get to the needed capacity we have decided to lure in standard farms and convert them to the organic path for free – our investment, not theirs. Second, or as a consequence of this lure, we will need to rejuvenate the soil; there's someone in Austria who can do this in weeks so we don't have to let the soil lie fallow for a long period of time. The biggest problem is pesticide residue. Some last for years: the neonicotinoid pesticide family residue half-life is up to 1,000 days. It's extremely toxic and you recall it wiped out the bees and was banned by the European Union (EU) in 2013, but only three out of seven kinds. The other pesticide used a lot is glyphosate and that's just been classified as a probable human carcinogen by the World Health Organisation. So they are really bad news. We need for all the pesticides to vanish from the soil and subsequently the potato harvest. That means we are going to be failing to meet our growth targets *and* have to pay these new farmers to basically do nothing for up to a year. Sounds like the EU doesn't it? And we have to give them an upfront financial incentive to attract them away from their current customers and farming methods.

Me: I read about the pesticides. It's hard to believe we are allowed to eat anything sprayed with them. So financially this could be bad news on the cash flow.

Joe: I'll say. It could wipe us out. But we are going ahead in pushing for us to convert new farms to organic so that we can continue to sell potatoes and over a one- to two-year period convert those farms to our way. In the long run it is the only way to farm.

Me: So you'll mix standard and organic potatoes?

Joe: No, we'll never sell non-organic. We may just not realise our short-term targets.

[Comment: The above describes potential conflicts between goals – the ideal of ethical farming in conflict with the expansion goal. This is something that Potato Grow will have to resolve and it will be the case that Potato Grow follows the proposal Joe puts forward to sell only organic produce. Selling non-organic produce is in direct conflict to their Environmental Strategy and there is a real risk they will be seen as moving away from organic in the market place. This runs a greater risk of loss of customers and reputation as well as causing environmental harm. This is a problem you need to explore a bit further.]

Me: If you sell non-organic potatoes – even over a short period of time whilst converting to organic – isn't there a risk you will harm your reputation as the leading organic potato supplier in the country?

Joe: Yes.

Me: How do you get round that?

Joe: We don't do it! We risk loss of some customers in the short term but we won't risk what is right.

Me: Who's in charge of the Environmental Strategy and implementation?

Joe: Abigail.

Me: Ah, she's on my list of interviewees but I wasn't sure of her role. I get to talk to her on Wednesday.

Joe: She'll know the ins and outs of it better than me.

Me: OK, let's move on. Tell me about the farm set up.

[Comment: I've changed tack because I need to get an idea of the current farming structure/operation. This question is essentially a lead in to discuss the supply chain, addressing Interview Objective 2: Identify structure of supply chain and proposed changes.]

Joe: Currently we are working with a very loose cooperative of potato farms and trying to get the farmers to cooperate in combining crops, as I mentioned. What we'd like to do is somehow get the farmers to work more closely together, offer incentives, centralise storage if we can.

Me: Are the farms located in the same region?

Joe: No, they aren't. We've got clusters dotted around the country.

Me: Do you have any centralised storage facilities now in any of the clusters?

Joe: Only in Brightmouth.

Me: How does that work now?

Joe: Really well. It reduces the overhead on the farmers in maintaining separate stores, provides a critical mass for medium to large orders and we have a better idea of the immediate available size of crop as it's all in one place.

Me: You want to be able to electronically check the stock size?

Joe: Initially, phone calls, email and then when the system is automated some kind of electronic monitoring such as a weighbridge idea. The potatoes are stored on what is a giant weighing scale or stored in specific cubic-sized boxes so we can calculate the weight straightaway. Orders come in by weight so we need to know that.

[Comment: We have some design options here and also some mechanisms for communication or interaction, that is, email, phone.]

Me: What about the supply chain? Talk me through how potatoes go from field to storage in this particular cluster and what happens when an order comes in.

Joe: Well, there are farming cycles that I'm not an expert on. Talk to Bill – he manages the direct relationship with the farmers. I'm more the logistics and customer-facing side. I'll get him to give you a call. You got a business card?

Me: Thanks, I did want to ask him a few questions. Here's the card.

Joe: Well, when an order comes in it will come to Peter's office. Pete is head of sales. He will pass this on to me in the usual way …

Me: The usual way?

Joe: Email the purchase order with delivery schedule. I'll check the local cluster to see if we can meet the order.

Me: How do you check you can meet the order?

Joe: I'll get one of my team to call the individual farmers, ask what amount and what variety is available, add up the amounts and get a total that way.

Me: How efficient is this?

Joe: It isn't, especially when farmers are out in their fields. That's why we really want to streamline crop quantity assessment to meet the large order request as rapidly as possible, faster than the order needs to be delivered if we can. I want to phone just one dedicated number at the cluster central storage site and get one correct and authorised answer instantly.

[Comment: Here's a key strategy–goal combination. The goal is to 'Meet the large order request sooner than the specified order delivery date' or words to this effect. The strategy to achieve this goal is: 'Streamline crop quantity assessment'. The partner responsible for this will be the supply chain department that Joe manages. The farm will partner in the achievement of these goals – we'll keep to the one term to keep it simple. What other partners might there be?]

Me: So how do you get the potatoes to the customer?

Joe: We have a number of supplier contractors we use in each region. We'll ring round until we can find one that's available when we want them to be.

Me: Can they handle significantly larger orders?

Joe: Maybe not. We've been a supporter of smaller businesses and our logistics providers are small businesses. Our orders until now have been small enough to fit in standard size trucks that most providers run. I don't think we have done the calculations on whether one truck will be able to carry a very large order. I will have to check on that. Good comment, thanks. We might have to use a larger logistics provider as they will be the only ones with the massive trucks that carry the big loads.

Me: So once the potatoes are loaded into the truck, what happens then?

Joe: They get taken to our sorting depot and quality checked.

Me: Oh? OK. So there's no quality checking done at the cluster?

Joe: No. At least right now there isn't. The sorting depot works really well. It extracts out the 5 to 8 per cent of potatoes that are rotten, too small or the wrong shape, plus removes all the earth and stones.

Me: How long does this take?

Joe: Once we get the potatoes there we can sift through 10 tons of potatoes an hour.

Me: How much is the average order in tons?

Joe: About 100 tons.

Me: So that's a whole day at the depot. What's the predicted large order going to be?

Joe: Anywhere from 1,000 to 2,000 tons.

Me: Where is the depot? Is it near the clusters?

Joe: No, we've only got one, just 10 miles from here.

Me: So, an order might come in from Brightmouth, the potatoes are sourced from your cluster near Brightmouth, you hire a logistics provider from Brightmouth to drive the potatoes here, about 150 miles, to be sorted and cleaned and then driven back 150 miles to Brightmouth the same day?

Joe: No, it's not the same day. Normally the turn around is two days to and from the depot.

Me: So it takes two days from pick up to delivery …

Joe: No, it is at least three days. One day to the depot, one day in the depot, one day from the depot. That part is quite slow. We want to be able to reduce the turnaround time of the potatoes from pick up to depot and back.

[Comment: Another goal: 'Reduce turnaround time of potatoes from pick up to depot and back'.]

Me: How reduced?

Joe: By about two days.

[Comment: This is a key performance indicator – reducing turnaround by two days. It's important to extract this sort of information for key goals because it allows you to focus on priorities and the client to set targets.]

Me: How do you plan to achieve that saving?

Joe: We're going to put localised depots at the cluster sites.

OK. So hopefully you get the idea. What you might like to do now is jump ahead to Chapter 4 and take a quick look at Tables 4.4 and 4.5. By following, more than less, the flowchart in Figure 3.1, you can quickly identify the goals, partners and their structure to quickly map out the strategic initiative. Of course, there is more to do than produce a table of relevant information from the interview and this is described in detail in Chapter 4. For now, though, the point has been to highlight what you can get out of the interview if you plan ahead and manage the interview well.

Hopefully you can see the pattern. Though the exact wording of questions is not predetermined, we have planned to cover a number of aspects and actually managed to find out exactly what we wanted to find. This has given us a platform to now consider the opportunities for process improvement and better practices. The analysis of this interview is discussed in Chapter 4.

## Wrap Up

When you are through the main event you will begin the wrap up process. You should have about five minutes left before the interviewee needs to be somewhere else. This is an opportunity for you to not bring the interview to an early close but to review the key points made by presenting what the interviewee said to you. You may also be able to check one or two extra points that you needed a bit more clarity on, or that the interviewee didn't answer, or that you didn't ask. Though this is in essence the next step in the interview lifecycle, there's no need for explicit demarcation in case the interviewee makes a run for it!

### WHAT NOT TO DO WHEN WRAPPING UP

Don't look at your watch and say, 'There's only five minutes to go and I don't understand anything you said … '[2] Don't aimlessly flip through your notepad to look for something to ask. Don't play back the recording of the interview in the hope of finding an unanswered question.

If you do any of these, the interviewee will leave the room and you will have lost an opportunity and left a bad impression.

### HOW TO WRAP UP EFFECTIVELY

As you have been conducting the interview, you will have made a few mental notes or jotted on your notepad the key points your interviewee made. The wrap up presents you an opportunity to reiterate those key points to ensure:

---

2   If you really didn't understand anything then you probably didn't do enough background work on context and ought to put in a few more days work before the next interview, if this is possible.

1. They *are* the key points.

2. The points are correct, according to the interviewee.

3. You interpreted the key points correctly (written down, recorded and/or in your head).

4. The interviewee has a chance to restate what really matters to him, what message he wants you to take away from this interview and pass on to others.

You should give the interviewee a summary question that repeats some of the key points the interviewee stated – you will need to skim through your mental and/or physical notes here but you will be doing so for a purpose and can say so as you skim.

Me: Joe, I just wanted to clarify one or two things about the environmental policy if that is OK?

Joe: Sure, no problem. I have five minutes then I have to be somewhere else.

Me: Ok, I'll keep it really short: what is the environmental policy?

Joe: Here's the official view and I like it … now if I can remember it. 'Potato Grow promises the earth that it will in no way harm its soil nor its sky not anything that lives and breathes between the two.' In other words, totally organic in everything we grow and use to grow.

[Comment: Here's the vital Environmental Vision that is pretty clear-cut. Will this cause a clash with the initiative goals?]

Me: That's the Vision?

Joe: The Environmental Vision, yes.

Me: I can see for farmers and farms that is already happening with the ethical farming practices I was told about …

Joe: That's right.

Me: And how will you manage to deal with supply chain on this?

Joe: Well, keeping everything in clusters will keep our carbon emissions lower as well as apply best environmental practices. The goal is a zero carbon footprint and if we have less distances to haul the potatoes then all the better. We expect our logistics to have fuel-efficient trucks.

[Comment: Details of how that Vision is achievable.]

Me: So you need to capture data about this?

Joe: Yes, we need to be ISO 16001 compliant in terms of the energy monitoring. We also need to be given certification by the Soil Association and the EU. We are already but we need to continue that practice.

[Comment: Specifics that make the initiative seem more and more difficult to achieve *if* these Environmental Goals are to be maintained and achieved.]

Me: How do you do that?

Joe: We measure the soil PH balance – well, they measure it – to determine if we are putting any unnatural chemicals on it or genetically engineered 'bug killers'. Our CEO is 100 per cent against that sort of chemical pollution and so are we and are farmers. We don't want that poison in our food supply.

[Comment: It is clear the environmental policy is not negotiable to the very top of the company, which is excellent but will mean some initiative goals may be frustrated. That is a price worth paying.]

Me: Is there a clash between this ethical farming and meeting your initiative targets?

Joe: Yes! We may not get within miles of our targets but we all believe it is better to do this than not. Listen, let's talk another time. I have to fly.

[Comment: Clear statement of priority here even if we see later that goals on both sides will clash.]

Me: Sure thing. Thank you, Joe.

Joe: You're welcome – this has been really good and I have your business card and you have mine …

You get the picture? You are sketching out the major points and presenting them back to the interviewee. If the interviewee says yes, then you've got the answer you were going to get. If no, the interviewee will enlighten you with more detail.

As I said at the start of this section, you might get a minute to ask a different question as a follow up to another point made by the interviewee if you didn't have the opportunity to follow up in the main event of the interview itself. If you believe it to be a really important point, go ahead and ask. If you think it really only minor, don't ask it even if curious. What you do next is set the scene for getting that information from your interviewee anyway in the warm down.

## Warm Down

Well done! You've reached the end of the interview. Hopefully the journey was pleasant and you followed some of the advice in Chapters 1 and 2 and in this chapter. Now is the moment to assess if you would like the opportunity for another meeting or would like to follow up with a few further questions via email.

The way you manage the warm down depends in large part on whom your interviewee is. If you are interviewing a senior manager who appears to be very knowledgeable about the subject you are investigating or appears to have a vested interest, it is a sensible idea to get the phone number and email of the manager's PA, assuming she has one and if not already offered.

If your interviewee is an operational-level employee who knows a little or a lot but that 'lot' is not of much interest, then you won't need to hand over your phone number. You will still need the interviewee's email address, which should be provided by your client's administrator if you don't already have it, because there is still a chance you will need to ask something. Don't give your email in return unless it is asked for. The same can be said of a high-level employee who has no relevance to the project. I interviewed someone like this on a project review. His reply to my opening question, 'Can you tell me about your role in this project?' went something like: 'I don't know much about this project as I had nothing to do with it but this is what I overheard in the corridor … ' I thought, uh oh. I probed a bit further and found out the employee had been in the company all of his working life, over 40 years, and simply had nothing to do even though in a senior role. He was part of the furniture and had always been there. I did not give my contact details to this person, nice a gentleman as he was.

To follow up or not to follow up? This depends upon a number of factors:

- What did you forget to ask or run out of time to ask?

- Is the person important enough to want to do so?

- What promises have been made by you or your employer regarding feedback?

- Are there further business opportunities that might come out of your interview? This does happen, believe me.

If you ran out of time, and assuming it was not your own fault, feel free to ask permission to follow up. It is quite straightforward. Just say something like this:

'There may be one or two points of clarity I might need to ask you once I've gone over my notes. Is it OK if I email you my questions? It shouldn't take more than 15 minutes of your time.'

Assuming the interview wasn't an absolute disaster and you didn't insult the interviewee, then the typical response you'll get is.

Interviewee: 'No problem at all. Do you have my email?'

## Summary

The point I want to make in this chapter with the example interview is that by planning ahead, finding out the context, and in setting interview objectives and questions to ask, you are more likely to elicit information that is really relevant to the engagement. It is acceptable to follow the flow of an interview so long as it is flowing in the right direction to meet your interview objectives and the engagement objective but without that upfront planning you may not know.

The interview itself is so important for you, the interviewee and your client. Your professionalism is on the line and exposed if you fall short. Planning will alleviate many of the shortfalls and proper execution should remove any concerns you, your interviewee and your client might have had.

Now the hard work is done, it's time to start the hard work and get on with the analysis.

# Chapter 4

# Interview Analysis

It isn't enough to have conducted a number of interviews, take everything at face value, slap it all into a document and then ask for your pay cheque there and then.

## SCENARIO: FAILURE TO CONDUCT ANALYSIS OF INTERVIEW FINDINGS

I was once on a project where a BA did exactly that. He held a series of interviews with stakeholders, wrote down everything they said and put it all together into a single specification document, without consideration of priorities, inconsistencies, errors or repetition. He'd gathered a lot of information but did not attempt to make any sense of it through even the most basic analysis. He even said it *wasn't* his job and was ultimately let go by the company who'd employed him – he was prophetic in a way, it *was* no longer his job.

The moral of the scenario is, if you've interviewed even only one person, you'll need to do a bit of analysis of that interview. Why?

1. To eliminate or highlight contradictions and conflicts.

2. To identify the most important points in respect of the engagement's overriding objective and interview objectives.

3. To identify the issues that come up again and again (not necessarily the same as the most important).

4. To be able to present the findings back to your client, and if needed the interviewee(s), in a coherent and engaging way by organising and structuring the findings potentially from a number of perspectives.

5. To help organise your own thoughts as you conduct more interviews or are reporting back on findings.

6.       To help validate interview findings with other interviewees.

The last two points indicate that it is wise to conduct analysis of your interviews as you progress through the engagement. It saves time, you learn more quickly and it feeds into your next interview either as validation or in reconsidering the questions you ask. It is also common that your client will expect an interim report either as an official document or more informally. This is unlikely to be written into your contract or proforma but it is normal procedure. Your client genuinely wants to know how you are progressing because she needs to have tangible beneficial results to: (1) convince her paymasters that the expense is worth it; (2) begin socialising your findings and recommendations with her colleagues; and (3) provide input and direction: are you still on the right track, who/what should you now avoid/include, are you on target timewise?

> Sometimes, your findings may not obviously be to the benefit all beings – but you should always set out to make the world a better place in its entirety.

The goal of analysis is to structure the information you have in such a way as to help you identify the right answers rapidly and effectively. Given you are working to a deadline, you also need to combine this with speed. There are many ways to conduct analysis but I've found the quickest and most expressive for our purposes are just two. One is a universally applicable, well-known, tried-and-tested analysis tool called content analysis. The second is less known and entirely different. It's the creation of a graphical model and is specifically employed in strategic initiatives. It is derived from the strategic alignment modelling framework originally developed by Steven Bleistein, June Verner and myself[1] and has been tried-and-tested in real engagements. This is the topic of Chapter 5. Remember this chapter is about analysis so the tools I present here are used in the context of conducting analysis on the interview data already gathered.

## Preparing to do Analysis

Before we get to the analysis there are a couple of things you need to do, and that is to transcribe the recording of the interview (if recorded) and/or read through your notes and write them up.

---

1    For example, Steven Bleistein, Karl Cox and June Verner (2006), Validating Strategic Alignment of Organisational IT Requirements using Goal Modeling and Problem Diagrams', *Journal of Systems and Software*, 79 (3), pp. 362–78.

There are a lot of tools on the market for transcription – voice recognition systems, for instance, where you 'train' the software to recognise your voice, and transcription service providers who for a fee will transcribe the recordings for you. My recommendation is to do it yourself the hard way or get your colleague who was in the interview with you to do the transcription. This means you need to transfer your recording from your recording device onto your computer first. Then you need to play back the recording and pause every few seconds to type what you hear into a document more or less word for word.

But isn't this very time consuming, not to mention boring? Yes, to both. But you gain enormously by revisiting your interview, confirming your initial opinions and quickly establishing where you have misunderstood something. Don't forget to consider the transcript with any notes you made on body language and/or emotions. Transcription is tedious but you learn so much about your interviewee and your engagement that it is worth the pain.

If you made notes or your colleague did, write these up as soon as possible into something legible. Then cross reference with the recording. You may find you have missed key words; for example, 'no', that would have given sentences such as the following an entirely different meaning:

'There are to be new services for customers over the next five years.'

I can transcribe a 50-minute interview in an hour if I am fast, sharp and keen. There comes a point, though, when tiredness descends and I begin ignoring chunks that are babble or what I consider to be not relevant. That's just the way it goes: if you have eight interviews, you will have eight hours of transcription, which is only a day's work ... though, as I said, I recommend you share the load with your colleague and transcribe each interview as soon as possible after it is over in order to maintain your sanity. Don't leave it all until the end.

Once you've transcribed an interview, or even during transcription, you should mark up the transcript as I have done with the example interview in Chapter 3. There's no need to provide explanations, just highlight strategies and partners if a strategic initiative or highlight root causes, symptoms and impacts if a post mortem review. Doing this will speed up the content analysis.

## Quick Content Analysis[2]

### BACKGROUND AND RATIONALE

There's full-blown scientifically rigorous content analysis[3] that is excellent for detailed research and then there's my watered down, quick and crude approach. Note this is not an attempt to invalidate rigorous scientific endeavour. In our context we simply do not have the time to take the full analytical approach. For us, it's just enough analysis to get a result that matters.

### HOW QUICK CONTENT ANALYSIS WORKS

Recall the interview was semi-formally guided by the flowchart in Figure 3.1 in Chapter 3. The flowchart not only helps structure the interview, it also acts as a pointer for the content analysis: you want to find out about strategies, goals and contexts (because this is the context of your engagement).

Another bonus of planning what you intend to ask is that you can draw a content analysis chart or table in advance so you can conduct a quick analysis of each interview as you go along even if the wording of the questions is different for different interviewees. Go through each interview transcript and add each answer into the content analysis table in its appropriate cell. You will need to paraphrase/summarise what people say. This is not a straightforward task because you will have to make connections and iron out contradictions that we always make as humans. Prioritise responses by counting similar responses and relating these to the overriding objective. You will have to decide what strategy receives priority. There are usually several goals and strategies that appear to be critical to those who are championing their personal preferences. When a strategic plan has already been set in stone – most government agencies will have a two-page glossy downloadable – for an outsider it is really difficult to work out what to do first and why. This is the opportunity to go back to your customer and find out what matters most.

---

2   Thanks to Christine Cox, my Mum, a successful consultant psychologist, for introducing me to this technique many years ago. The version of content analysis described here was taught by the Open University. The original work on content analysis is quite old and a key reference dates back to 1952: Bernard Berelson, *Content Analysis in Communication Research*, Glencoe, Ill: Free Press 1952.

3   For example, Kimberly Neuendorf, *The Content Analysis Guidebook*, Thousand Oaks, CA, Sage Publications 2002.

Stakeholders will have different degrees of importance. This must be balanced with relevance. So you can't simply agree that everything the CEO said was the most important. The CEO will know the strategy but when it comes to implementation of a strategy on the factory floor, it will be the shop floor managers and specialist engineers who will know what is most important to do and when. Conversely, they will have only a restricted idea of their company's strategy, which is not always good enough.

Begin analysis by conducting a content analysis on the interview material. But if you've interviewed 20 to 30 people or more, doing all that analysis will kill the project – you will suffer paralysis. So now is the time to remember your planning from Chapter 1 on prioritising stakeholders: who are the key stakeholders, why? You may not be so fortunate as to be able to prioritise stakeholders but if you are, good.

Note, for a strategic initiative engagement, it is possible to get skewed responses because the number of individual interviewees per role will vary quite a bit. You might get to interview only one executive and two general managers but talk with 15 operational managers, four end users, three BAs and a sole customer representative. You are unlikely to ask the same question of an end user as that of a general manager. Nonetheless, plotting responses in this table format makes a difference to your analysis and interpretation of findings. If you are conducting a post mortem review you may find you are repeating many questions whoever the interviewee is. You'll also have specific questions for that interviewee's role.

There is a lack of scientific rigour and there's a seriously good reason for this. You are running against a clock and you have to deliver a good result. Scientists and researchers often have more time to pursue the absolutes or perfect result. The world of consulting and business analysis is not a scientific laboratory. So you have to make do with good enough and hope this is convincing enough. By planning your interviews, running them effectively and conducting quick but expressive analysis, you are going to present a convincing storyline.

## AN EXAMPLE OF HOW TO DO CONTENT ANALYSIS (AS TABLE 4.1)

Remember Table 2.2 where I presented different viewpoints on the same question? Here it is again:

**Table 4.1    Table 2.2 revisited: Getting viewpoints**

| Role | Question | Possible Responses |
|------|----------|--------------------|
| Chief information officer | How is IT supporting the increase market share business strategy? | Pretty well aligned, we've just implemented a new sales management system for sales staff to support their operations. This is now fully integrated into the inventory management system in the warehouse and the CRM the help support desk people are using. |
| Sales manager | How well does the new management system support and report on your drive to attract new customers and get more sales of new products? | The new system is really great for reporting. We can now keep track of the number of product sales and can keep the warehouse up to date on anticipating stock level requirements. So we can count the number of new customers easily and they've gone up by 12 per cent for this quarter compared to this time last year. |
| Customer help desk operator | Has the new CRM system you're using helped you in doing your job in solving customer problems or dealing with their complaints? | No, I find it takes too long to find a customer record and it doesn't show any of their purchase details. So when a customer rings in to complain that their product is faulty or they are having difficulties in setting it up or a part is missing, I really want to see what they ordered in case the warehouse team have put any notes already about product defects and fixes I can quickly recommend. The old paper system worked like that – you just had to go through the pile to get to the right one and match it with the sales record on the old sales system. |
| Warehouse manager | Does the inventory management system get updated automatically now that the sales and CRM systems are integrated with it? | It works brilliantly except that the updates come in as soon as a product has been purchased. The problem with this is that the system automatically sends the supplier a purchase order for the next product. What if we don't want to use that supplier any more or they've gone out of business or they don't stock that product anymore? We used to keep all requests for new products and send them in a weekly batch once we had talked to our suppliers on the phone. It might seem old fashioned but that call made all the difference as the supplier could tell us what was working for them, what they anticipated as coming in next from the manufacturer. Now we've lost that human touch and sometimes our purchase orders are unanswered and more often than not, a supplier will get fed up with the continual orders and call us up moaning why we can't send a batch once a week like we used to. All the supplier does now is collect all the orders and at the end of the week bundle them off as one order to the manufacturer anyway. Trouble is with all those individual orders the supplier can lose some of the paperwork and we come up short on products – it happens all the time. This is really bad when the demand is high. |

| Role | Question | Possible Responses |
|------|----------|--------------------|
| Customer representative | When you buy a new product have you noticed any change in the service you get? | I can use more credit cards now as I can order online if I want. That's pretty good and the website is really informative and easy to use. The help desk isn't that helpful – they can't ever track down my last order if I have a problem or question about it. That seems to be happening more and more and it is really frustrating. |

Content analysis works in more or less the same way. You are looking from different viewpoints for commonalities in response. It is unlikely you will be able to ask exactly the same question each time to different stakeholders because you have to word the question in the language of the individual interviewee as determined by their role.

Next, we rephrase and restructure Table 4.1 to show how content analysis is done. The important thing to remember in Table 4.2 is that this is meant to be quick because time is always short. So we have to accept a degree of interpretation on your part as BA or consultant. To be honest, your employer will expect your take on the issues at hand and discuss or present your take on it. This is why you really have to know the context of the engagement.

Note that when you set out to draw up a table like Table 4.2, you are better off doing it manually. Use A3 or poster-size paper, assuming a reasonable number of interviewees and questions. If you've interviewed several people in the same role, for example, 15 customer service staff, put these interviewees onto the same sheet of paper. Don't forget to use coloured highlighter pens or whatever way works best for you to highlight similarities. Here the table is in black and white but uses references numbers (1), (2) and so on. You can use different fonts and colours also to help the key similarities stand out further. The good thing with using paper, as opposed to a software application, is that you really have to think about summarising answers to questions because you have finite space to work with and you also have to be very clear in your interpretation of what your interviewees say. Once you've got a draft you might then want to put it all into electronic format.

Did you remember to highlight strategies, goals and contexts on the interview transcriptions? Good, because doing that makes the next step quicker and easier. You can now populate answers to the questions in Table 4.2 much faster because you've done a lot of the identification work already.

Table 4.2    Content analysis extending example from Table 4.1

| Question / Role | Q1. Has technology successfully supported a business strategy of increasing market share by 25 per cent by successfully selling a range of new products? | Q2: What direction should the business take over the next three years to achieve the market growth target? | Q3: What else do you need to do to hit the 25 per cent market share? | Q4: What risks do you see in the drive to hit the growth target? |
|---|---|---|---|---|
| Chief information officer | (1) Yes, new sales management system fully integrated into the inventory management system and CRM for help desk. | We need to (3) refresh our infrastructure. We have a new integrated system in place now but the underlying infrastructure is a problem. We also need to be 100 per cent online. | Need to measure performance. (4) Iron out a few operational issues. Big one: (3) refresh infrastructure – it is 20 years old and crumbling. | The Board won't support infrastructure refresh as they don't see it as strategic. But without that refresh won't deliver a good result and will impact negatively on target. |
| Sales general manager | (1) Yes, now keep track of product sales and keep the warehouse up to date on anticipated stock level requirements. New customers up by 12 per cent for this quarter compared to this time last year. | Currently we are selling through outlets more than online, though there's a shift to online. 100 per cent online good target. | Better marketing! IT support getting to be a problem: old, ugly and slow. Need to change it if we are going 100 per cent online. | Product quality may suffer as we try to blitz sell. (6) If we close all outlets, we could alienate many customers. Could push away 10–20 per cent of existing customer base. Have to review outlets vs online. Rebranding to online might confuse or put off customers. |
| Customer help desk operator | (2) No, takes too long to find a customer record and there are no purchase details. If a customer complains about a product it is not possible to see what they ordered in the case that the warehouse team have put any notes about product defects and fixes to recommend. | We need to really integrate the systems that deal with the customer. Right now I log onto three different systems: CRM, warehouse inventory and accounts to provide one answer. It takes too long. We should integrate them. | Need a better incident and problem process – right now it is ad hoc. Need an (3) integrated system that works and doesn't crash. | Lack of staff. No one has talked about increasing staff numbers to deal with extra anticipated calls. (7) If IT not fixed then we are going to fail. (6) Online might put off customers who like the human touch? |

| | | | |
|---|---|---|---|
| Warehouse manager | (1) Yes, (2) but the inventory system automatically sends the supplier a purchase order for the next product immediately. Want weekly batch once agreed with suppliers. Lost human touch. Risk purchase orders can go unanswered/missing or supplier complains about stream of purchase orders – wants a weekly batch. | Online better solution. Cost less to have just one centralised warehouse. Right now we have 20 outlets with 20 small warehouses plus a central one – here: expensive. One warehouse also means smaller number of logistics providers: cheaper. Fix the inventory management system with help desk and suppliers: batch orders on a weekly basis. | Either fix the old systems as they are old or (3) fix the new system so it does what we want. Better to do both but I don't know if we can afford it. (5) Centralise the warehouse, (4) simplify the supply chain and logistics. | We need to rethink our processes to handle the extra volume. If we do centralise we need to start now – it will take a year to get right. I think the executive is too obsessed on the nice looking online shop front that there's a danger of not providing the back end support: lean warehouse, supplier and logistics practices. |
| Customer representative | (1) Yes, there are more products (2) but also problems for us: the help desk can't track down order if there is a problem. | I'm happy with online orders these days and so are my fellow customers. We're using outlets only 60 per cent of the time now and that's dropped from 95 per cent a year ago. | Good customer support at the help desk. Bigger range of products but keep the quality up. | Don't pass on cost of change to us as price hikes. (6) Worried that loss of real face-to-face contact will lower standards and customer service – assuming it gets fixed. |

*Question 1:* Note that I have indicated (1) positive and (2) negative responses. I've only indicated 'yes' and 'no'/'but' responses to give me a rough head count for this point. You can clearly see there is some satisfaction from the CIO and the sales general manager, and even a modicum of support from the warehouse manager, so that strategically there appears to be some benefit from the technology transformation. The customer representative is happy about having more product options. But there are also negatives: the customer help desk operator has issues with the system operationally – it takes too long to get a customer record and it isn't possible to see fixes. The warehouse manager, though supportive of technology change, is now finding the relationship with his suppliers becoming strained because orders are no longer batched, causing extra unnecessary work for both the warehouse and the suppliers. The customer representative, like the customer help desk operator, is frustrated that it takes so long to find the customer order and purchase information.

So to put an answer, and your own spin, to Question 1, it's clear there is a mixed message. Yes, market share does appear to be up, but not to the level anticipated. So strategically our client is on the right path. However, the executive needs to be aware of some operational problems with the warehouse purchase order system and CRM system. Both are failing their staff, suppliers and customers. Your recommendation here would be to fix these problems: (i) batch purchase orders to suppliers on a weekly basis as before; (ii) integrate the warehouse system with the CRM so help desk staff can see product fixes and recommendations; and (iii) speed up/fix customer purchase record access on the CRM so the help desk can provide a better service and customers are happier.

*Question 2:* There's a clear desire to go online in order to grow the business. We knew this from answers to Question 1 and the answers here reinforce this. Four of the five interviews stated that online was important though the customer representative said customers were happy with online buying, 60 per cent of purchases were still done at outlets. The customer help desk operator and the warehouse manager realise that there are 'problems with the new integrated system that need to be fixed' to provide a better service for customers. The only other strategy to emerge was for a (3) refresh of the infrastructure as suggested by the CIO.

It's clear what you need to recommend to your client: go online to grow the business. But there are some problems that have to be addressed, perhaps with more urgency than the online solution. The CIO claims a successful roll out of an integrated system to manage stock and customer sales. But (4) operationally there are some concerns that will need to be fixed to improve performance. Also, a worrying development for the whole company is the state of its technical infrastructure. If the infrastructure fails then none of its services will succeed. Perhaps, then, an equal strategy to match online in importance is an infrastructure refresh. Of course, this will have to be explored further to ascertain the current state of the infrastructure and its implications for the business and existing and planned technologies.

*Question 3:* Asks what else needs to be done to achieve 25 per cent market share. Naturally, all interviewees had much to say and much of it was diverse. However, the same two themes were expressed three times:

- (3) fix the new integrated system to remove some operational concerns;

- fix the IT support, that is, an (3) infrastructure refresh.

The next most recurrent topic was to provide better management of customers at the help desk. The customer representative called this 'good customer support' and the help desk operator called this better 'incident and problem management'.

In preparing a consolidated answer to this question, the best approach is to list the most frequent occurrences as shown. Do not ignore the single entries because within the scope of the interviewee's responsibilities, the single entry might be vital to success. The warehouse manager was adamant that a (5) centralised warehouse was *the* way forwards for an online-only strategy. Perhaps no one else would be likely to propose this strategy because they simply would not know. The worst thing to do would be to discard this opinion on the grounds that no one else had the same idea. Again, you have to know your context in order to understand the importance of this interviewee.

*Question 4:* There are always downsides to an upside or strategy. It is important to know what these are and manage them through the strategic initiative or change. The most recurrent concern is the potential negative (6) impact on customers of loss of face-to-face contact as everything goes online. This concern was raised three times. The next most recurrent was a risk that the IT infrastructure won't be fixed. There are a number of significant individual concerns that need to be addressed as well. Again, I would consider who the interviewee is and whether that person is speaking from an authoritative position. Clearly, the warehouse manager should be concerned that processes will not be adequately changed to efficiently deliver the new online business model. These are things you need to make absolutely clear as a BA/consultant.

## BENEFITS OF CONTENT ANALYSIS

I hope the above example makes the task of content analysis straightforward, though not necessarily easy, and shows how important a tool it is in your daily job. The first thing of note, other than the use of different fonts and highlighting or colours, is that it very soon becomes obvious what the recurring points are that interviewees make, not just individually but across a group of often disparate people. In the above example, the CIO and the warehouse manager are strong advocates for going online. This strategy is also supported by the customer representative though with a touch of caution. You should also be wary that high recurrence of a comment does not necessarily mean that it is a high priority in the greater scheme of things. Your job is to determine what is best for the business and its customers, not always to fix the niggles. But you should take note of it in case it is a symptom of a larger problem.

Content analysis quickly shows you what was missed. You may find that a key interviewee has not answered an important question either because you did not ask it or because it was misinterpreted or only brushed upon in order to make another point but not returned to. The gap is easy to identify because it is a white space on an otherwise text-laden, and if in colour, colourful grid.

A subsequent benefit is that you can take the answers given and model them. In other words, if you are conducting a strategic initiative engagement where you are trying to establish key strategies for an organisation over the next three years, you can use content analysis to highlight what strategies are recurrent among the different roles. This will allow you to build a visual model of the 'consensus' view of the organisation's strategic direction. 'Consensus' may not be the best path but it is a starting point for discussion. How to build a strategic model is discussed in the next chapter.

Note the content analysis presents a lot of rich information on just the one page as seen in Table 4.2. You can see the value of this approach. Identifying the goals, strategies, tactics and partners, or root causes, impacts, symptoms and opportunities if a post mortem review, from the content analysis is relatively quick. Remember this is not a scientific study; it is a business engagement or assignment and you are probably a consultant or BA or student working to tight deadlines. There is no doubt you could conduct a more complete analysis of those interview transcripts but you don't want to run out of time and deliver very little. The content analysis provides a quick and dirty approach to organising interview answers, which is exactly what you need in your situation.

## Strategic Initiative Analysis: Potato Grow Ltd

If you recall from Chapter 3, I mention that it is a good idea to try and identify strategies, goals, tactics and business partners. Take another look at the interview with Joe, the Director of Supply Chain and Customer Relations and leading the strategic initiative at Potato Grow. Note my comments on identifying goals and partners. What if I did this for a number of interviews? How would I be able to determine the key strategies, goals and business partners? Yes, you've guessed it, we can do a content analysis of those interviews. Table 4.3 shows the results:

Table 4.3    Content analysis of Potato Grow interviews

| Question / Role | Q1. What is the Vision for the strategic initiative? | Q2. What key goals do you have to achieve to support that Vision and who/what is involved in that? | Q3. What do you need to do to achieve those goals in Q2? | Q4. Who is going to be involved in hitting those targets, strategies and goals (Q3)? |
|---|---|---|---|---|
| Joe, Supply Chain Director; Initiative Director | (1) To increase potato supply to meet and exceed the projected demand over (2) the next five years. | (4) Be ready to supply European market – Potato Grow and EU customers; (6) deliver on large orders faster than agreed delivery date – Potato Grow and local customers; Provide centralised storage of potatoes on farms; (7) monitor crops and potato availability to meet large orders. | (3) Goal: increase potato capacity by 200 per cent within 12 months; (10) Strategy: streamline crop quantity assessment; (12) Goal: reduce potato quality assessment time by two days. | Us: supply chain department, working with the potato farms individually and also managing farms as clusters. Farms will reduce quality assessment time by doing assessment in-house. |
| Abigail, Environmental Director | (1) To continuously meet the potato demand through high-quality efficient sales (2) over the next five years. | (6) Deliver on large orders faster both EU and here, Potato Grow as a whole is taking on this responsibility for its customers. (5) Farms have to be capable of increasing capacity. | Build a sales operation that encompasses our key EU partners; (11) make sure our logistics is efficient and economical; (3) increasing potato capacity by 200 per cent. | Sales division to build the sales operation; EU partners to manage EU office; logistics providers to get that right; farms to increase capacity. |
| Bill, Director Supplier Relations | (1) To improve potato supply to meet projected increases in demand over (2) the next five years. | (4) Establish foothold in EU market; be ready for the EU market; Potato Grow, customers, farms, logistics providers. (5) Cluster farms to bring crops together to ensure critical mass in order to meet increased demand. | We will need to (11) implement supply efficiencies to meet growing demand. | Individual farms have to be convinced by Potato Grow executive to join a cluster. Logistics providers will need to rethink their current strategy. |

| | | | |
|---|---|---|---|
| CIO | (1) To meet potato demand without the use of smart and mobile technologies. | (8) Establish a technical infrastructure and applications for (7) monitoring potato supply and readiness. IT dept, farms, sales, logistics providers. | (13) Assess current process of entire potato lifecycle to understand where IT fits and adds value. (14) Implement an infrastructure within two years; apps on top within next year so whole system running by end of year 3. Need two years operation to determine return on investment (ROI) rate. | IT dept in charge but we need to know the business of other aspects of Potato Grow to make sure we only change what we have to. So they will be: sales, supply chain, supplier relations, logistics, farms. |
| Potato farmer cluster representative | No idea but there's a push to consolidate potato farms (1) to meet a growing demand. | (5) Bring together crop storage and assessment under one roof to increase capacity and bring efficiency; ensure farmers get a good deal; (9) guarantee business or sustainable income. | (16) Plan phased change to not disrupt current business; (15) produce a contract to guarantee relationships between farmers and Potato Grow remain good. | Individual farms, farmers and Potato Grow (both). |

Table 4.3    continued

| Question / Role | Q5. PG has a reputation for being environmentally friendly. Could you describe the environmental policy? | Q6: What key goals and strategies do you have to achieve to support that Environmental Vision? | Q7: Who is responsible for achieving those Environmental Goals and Strategies and how do you measure their success? | Q8: What is the impact on the strategic initiative of the environmental policy? |
|---|---|---|---|---|
| Joe, Supply Chain Director; Initiative Director | Always organically grown potatoes. New mantra more extreme: (17) 'Potato Grow promises the earth that it will in no way harm its soil nor its sky nor anything that lives and breathes between the two'. | I think the big goals are (18) 'Carbon zero carbon footprint'. So no pollution. That means a lot more than being organic. We have to have to (19) continue ethical farming practices, (20) apply environmental best practice in our clusters, (21) reduce emissions in our logistics and supply chain, (22) get more farmers. | We are. I guess the farms and farmers will be responsible for the ethical farming and we will oversee or monitor this. We will have to (23) capture emissions data, (24) measure the soil PH balance? Rejuvenate the soil. | (27) Conflict between the Environmental Vision and the initiative Vision? Ethical farming might mean we cannot get anywhere near our 200 per cent increase in crop target. Goal of being more efficient in logistics/ transport and tactic of examining supply chain to identify these negatively impacted by strategy of reducing emissions in our logistics? |
| Abigail, Environmental Director | Our Vision. I composed it: (17) 'Potato Grow promises the earth that it will in no way harm its soil nor its sky nor anything that lives and breathes between the two.' | (18) Reduce carbon footprint to zero across the business – farms, operations, transport; (19) continue ethical farming: no GMO, no chemicals; (22) recruit more ethical farmers; (20) apply best environmental practice to clusters to bring efficiencies. | All of us at PG, farmers, logistics providers. We will (23) capture emissions data through automated meter reading in terms of gas/electric. Try (26) to reduce fugitive gas emissions. (24) Measure soil acidity and nutrients. | All positive. Ethical farming supports farmers in getting a good deal – they can trust us to keep farms organic. Helps us recruit new farms for the clusters. Applying best environmental practices helps in the phased change in expanding our business. |

| | | | |
|---|---|---|---|
| Bill, Director Supplier Relations | We've been environmentally friendly but now we've set a bit of a Vision: (17) 'We will in no way harm the earth or anything on it' or something akin to that. | (18) Zero carbon footprint. (21) Check that logistics have low emissions. Reuse farm waste for energy? Don't know if we have got that far yet. | Abigail is driving this backed by the CEO. Joe's keen as well. The farmers themselves will have to do most of the work and we'll monitor. Not sure how this is done. Ask Abigail. |
| | | | (27) Could be a disaster as we will focus on two different things rather than one. Good reputation for organically grown produce. (27) Becoming more environmentally extreme risks losing focus on saving business. |
| CIO | We are keen to be seen as green. And we have always been that. Now we to want to conquer the world in natural farming: (17) don't harm the planet and so on. | The usual stuff: (18) carbon neutral at PG; (19) ethical farming; (21) transport with low emissions – run on chip fat oil! Ironic but smart. | Abigail is driving this. PG will have to take ultimate responsibility. (23) Measure our energy usage? We don't monitor this now so will have to introduce some system! (24) Level of soil toxification? |
| | | | (27) Conflict between environmental direction and efficiency drive. Have to keep customers happy first then worry about saving the planet. But got to remain organic and ethical. |
| Potato farmer cluster representative | Heard about the new mantra. All good. We are organic and ethical farmers: no GMO, no pesticides, no chemicals. We farmers love Potato Grow! | We are already organic farmers. We (20) could improve what we do but we are doing a good job. Heard stories about (18) carbon neutral though and making sure (19) we remain ethical, organic farmers: we do this anyway because we believe in it. | Farmers! We (24) already monitor the quality of the soil and we also (25) maintain the ideal of countryside: hedgerows and copses for insects and birds, wild flowers for bees, co-cropping with cash crop for greater water retention, letting fields lie fallow and go wild – we are already ethical. |
| | | | No idea. They want more potatoes but ethical farming is natural farming so we don't use artificial feeds, pesticides on principle. If they want more potatoes, get more farms. The cluster works better than separate farms. Cluster more farms. |

Table 4.3 shows all goals, strategies, tactics and partners identified from the interviews for eight questions; four relate to the strategic initiative and four to the new environmental policy and its impact on the initiative. Remember to keep in mind the engagement objective: to independently validate the strategic initiative that Potato Grow has conceived, to identify and highlight any inconsistencies there might be and make recommendations for improvements. Also, consider the key questions per interview. This will give you a sense of the goal priorities. You'll be happy you did that planning as described in Chapters 1 and 2 because this makes life easier now. For Joe, our interview objectives are:

1.    identify key strategies and Vision for initiative;

2.    identify structure of supply chain and proposed changes;

3.    understand the potential conflicts in initiative against environmental policy.

Let's go through each question to explain the annotated points.

*Question 1:* You might think it unusual to ask about an initiative's Vision because this is nearly always set in stone and many senior employees can quote it. Whether they all have the same interpretation of it is another matter so that's why I tend to ask it. As you can see from the responses, each has a different take on the same theme as determined by their role and their understanding of the initiative. That theme is to (1) grow/meet/improve potato supply to meet anticipated growth in demand. Three of the five interviewees also mentioned a (2) five-year time frame. But here we note there is a possible goal conflict and this refers to the time frames for implementation. Though three interviews note the five-year time frame in answer to Question 1, this does seem to be in conflict with Joe's answer to Question 3 where he suggests as a key goal (3) a 12-month time frame for increasing crop capacity by 200 per cent. Is this really a contradiction? If so, how do we deal with this? We should consider if these goals really are in conflict; it is possible that the 12-month time frame is just the first step to achieving the five-year Vision. Given that the current infrastructure is not sufficient to support a 200 per cent increase in capacity it might be safe to assume that this figure is a bit beyond the realms of reasonableness. In this case, I would go back to Joe and ask for more details and clarification. Is the target short term or long term? Is the short-term achievement in capacity increase necessary in order to achieve the five-year Vision? What happens after we hit the 200 per cent increase in capacity? Do we need to double the capacity again over the next 12 months? What if the infrastructure is not in place to hit this target?

Do we need the entire infrastructure in place to get even a 10 per cent increase or is a 50 per cent increase going to be good enough? In other words, is it possible to deliver a piece of the infrastructure and get the returns needed or do we have to do everything before any return can be seen? What happens if we miss the target? These are crucial questions that must be answered honestly if Potato Grow is going to meet its strategic Vision. You'll need to ask but first revisit the interview transcript. After another look at Joe's interview, it seems there is not a conflict but that this 12-month deadline is the first key step in moving towards achievement of the Vision. Check with Joe, anyway.

Given that the majority of interviewees provided a similar view of the strategic Vision, we ought to consolidate those to deliver an agreed and shared Vision. When this is done, place the Vision statement into the business strategy, Table 4.4. Whether this is the final agreed Vision remains to be seen but it is taking a step towards that shared understanding. The purpose of Table 4.4 is two-fold: (i) to maintain a single document that lists all the goals, strategies and tactics alongside those partners responsible for them or impacted by their achievement; and (ii) the completed table serves as a guide for creating a graphical strategy model.

*Question 2:* Each interviewee will have an idea about key goals – what is it that Potato Grow wants to achieve? – and which business partners are responsible for or involved in that achievement? This means that consolidation suddenly becomes more difficult. However, at a strategic level, the key goals should be reasonably clear, though focussed on different business units.

The most repeated goals in answer to Question 2 are to (4) be ready to supply the EU market (Goal 1 in Table 4.4) followed by (5) improving potato capacity and efficiencies (Goal 3) for (6) faster delivery on larger orders (Goal 2) by centralising and putting them under one roof. Goal 3 does not directly contribute to the Vision but to Goals 1 and 2. The CIO and Joe both recommend a strategy of (7) monitoring potato and supplier readiness (Strategy 3 in Table 4.4) that is achieved by (8) establishing the technical infrastructure (Tactic 1). Though this tactic comes from the CIO alone, this is key point because it will be very difficult to know if Potato Grow is hitting its targets without the infrastructure to support achievement of those targets.

The potato farmer representative provides a different perspective on what Potato Grow needs to do to get farmer buy-in: ensure farmers get a good deal (Goal 4, which helps achieve the Vision) implemented through Strategy 4: (9) guarantee business/sustainable income. It's important to document these though they may have nothing to do with technology; Potato Grow will fail very fast in its initiative if it does not get farmer buy-in and put practices in place to keep farmers happy.

*Question 3:* Note that we are getting more concrete in terms of what goals are supposed to be achieved. Question 3 asks what needs to be done, primarily as strategies and tactics to achieve those goals as described in answer to Question 2. One response that occurs twice is absolutely explicit about its intent and time frame: *(3) Increase potato crop capacity by 200 per cent within 12 months* (Goal 5 in Table 4.4). Note this is bold and italicised. This is a reminder that there is potential for conflict between this goal and the longer Vision of five years as stated in response to Question 1. It's flagged as something we need to check. Goal 5 is supported by Strategy 5: (10) streamline crop quantity assessment.

Tactic 2: (11) implement supply chain and logistics efficiencies is a combination of two responses, one regarding the supply chain and the other logistics. I've made logistics explicit in order to keep both parties, sales and supplier relations engaged. They are not directly involved but they are aware. This supports Strategy 3.

There's another tactic to support a strategy. Build a sales operation that encompasses key EU partners to meet growing demand (Tactic 5 supporting Strategy 1).

Joe states another goal of (12) reducing potato quality assessment time frames by two days (Goal 8). This contributes the achievement of Goal 3.

The CIO suggests Tactic 3 to (13) assess current process for the entire potato lifecycle in order to contribute to the achievement of Goal 6, (14) implement an infrastructure within two years and applications within three years. This obviously makes sense because there's no point setting targets for rolling out an IT infrastructure and applications without that initial assessment: you would have no starting point of reference.

In order to maintain good farmer relations, (15) Potato Grow should produce a contract to guarantee relationships between themselves and the farmers (Goal 7). As part of a successful implementation of Strategy 4, Potato Grow should (16) plan a phased change without disrupting current business (Tactic 4) for itself and for the farms.

*Question 4:* Highlights the business partners who are responsible for or influenced by the strategies, goals and tactics from Question 3. It's vital to know who is responsible for each goal, strategy and tactic because that makes them accountable. It is also entirely sensible to place any goal or requirement you may have within a context.

Transitioning from the content analysis to a structure as in Table 4.4 provides you with a log of strategic goals and responsibilities. You may find you iterate between the raw interview data in the transcripts, the content analysis and Table 4.4 to ensure you have got everything documented correctly. This is a perfectly normal approach that I recommend you take to ensure you have represented your customers' views accurately. The additional benefit of Table 4.4, as I mentioned, is that it provides you with a structure to quickly construct a strategic model to represent the same information in a visual way. This is described in the next chapter but for now let us take a look at Table 4.4.

**Table 4.4    Business strategy table: Potato Grow strategic initiative**

| Business Strategy | Main Partner | Supporting Partners | Helps Achieve |
|---|---|---|---|
| **VISION** | | | |
| V: Ready to meet increases in potato demand over the next five years. | Potato Grow | — | — |
| **Goals** | | | |
| G1: Capability to supply EU market. | Potato Grow | EU market | V |
| G2: Faster delivery on large orders. | Potato Grow | Customers | V |
| G3: Combine crops into one place to increase capacity and efficiency. | Farms | Potato Grow | G2 |
| G4: Ensure farmers get a good deal. | Potato Grow | Farmer | V |
| G5: Increase potato crop capacity by 200 per cent within 12 months. | Potato Grow | Farms | G3 |
| G6: Implement an infrastructure within two years; applications by end of year 3. | IT dept | Potato Grow, farms, logistics, supply chain, sales, supplier relations | G3 |
| G7: Produce a contract to guarantee relationships between farmers and Potato Grow remain good. | Potato Grow | Farmers | G4 |
| G8: Reduce potato quality assessments by two days. | Farms | Potato Grow | G3 |

**Table 4.4**     *continued*

| Business Strategy | Main Partner | Supporting Partners | Helps Achieve |
|---|---|---|---|
| **Strategies** | | | |
| S1: Establish high-quality efficient sales process. | Sales | Customers, EU market | G1, G2 |
| S2: Avoid use of smart and mobile technologies.[4] | IT dept | Potato Grow | G1, G2 |
| S3: Monitor potato supply and readiness. | IT dept | Farms, sales, logistic providers | G3 |
| S4: Guarantee business/sustainable income. | Potato Grow | Farmer | G4 |
| S5: Streamline crop quantity assessment. | Potato Grow | Farms | G8 |
| **Tactics** | | | |
| T1: Establish technical infrastructure. | IT dept | Farms, sales, logistic providers | S3 |
| T2: Implement supply chain and logistics efficiencies. | Supply chain | Logistics providers, customers | S3 |
| T3: Assess current process for entire potato lifecycle. | IT dept | Potato Grow, farms, logistics, supply chain, sales, supplier relations | G6 |
| T4: Plan phased change to not disrupt current business. | Potato Grow | Farms | S4 |
| T5: Build a sales operation that encompasses key EU partners. | Sales | EU market, customers | S1 |

Note that the goals, strategies and tactics in Table 4.4 are not an exact match to those elicited from Joe in his interview in Chapter 3. This is to be expected because Table 4.4 is drawn from five interviews as shown in the content analysis. As such there is a degree of consolidation in getting the language right in the business strategies in Table 4.4 and also in structuring the strategic model. It is not always correct to assume that the initiative leader is absolutely right about everything on the project; farmers should know more about running farms than supply chain managers, for instance. So where strategies and goals revolve around the farm part of the initiative, it makes sense to get the expert opinion direct from the farmer; this means you might have to rephrase a goal to put it in the language and context of that stakeholder.

---

4    This is a somewhat strange strategy, you might think. But Potato Grow have become aware that manmade microwave technology is causing the worldwide disappearance of the bees. The CIO pointed me to this source which sums up the research on this: *The World Foundation for Natural Science* (October 2014) 'The worldwide disappearance of the bees', http://www.naturalscience.org/publications/the-worldwide-disappearance-of-the-bees/ accessed 20 July 2015. Hence it is important to Potato Grow to avoid technology that is harming the natural environment.

It may seem something of a leap of faith to go from the looseness of content analysis to the structure of Table 4.4. But there is a way to populate this table with some degree of rigour. Remember the flow diagram in Figure 3.1? If you follow the steps through this flow diagram, it presents you with a step-by-step structure in how to construct the table and, later on, a goal-context model. So the first thing to consider in the flow diagram is who owns the initiative. That's actually quite simple because it ought to be the organisation you are working with. In this case, it is Potato Grow. We add their name to the column, 'main partner'. Next step is to consider what the owner wants to achieve overall. This becomes the Vision statement and is entered into the 'business strategy' column of the table in the same row. The next questions are to identify who the owner works with to achieve the Vision and how they do that. I have found it often easier to list all the partners and all the goals, strategies and tactics than systematically identify partner then goal then contribution in hierarchy. People's minds work better when listing like-minded things, in general. So we would look at what partners will work with Potato Grow: EU market, customers, farmers and so on. Then we will consider what they do to contribute to the achievement of the Vision. We decide on which partner takes ultimate responsibility or drives the achievement of the particular goal or strategy or tactic. The last step is to address the 'helps achieve' column. We decide what goals, strategies and tactics are really supporting others or are more concrete expressions of others. There is no magic formula for this. It is done by detective work driven through communicating with your clients and interviewees. To add a degree of readability to the table, I have placed the goals, the strategies and the tactics in separated sections.

Don't forget we need to also consider the Environmental Goals and Strategies as identified in the interview with Joe and confirmed in subsequent interviews as highlighted in the content analysis. Shouldn't we add those into the Table 4.4? After all, we are talking about goals and strategies. If we think for a minute about the environmental policy of the company, this is something that will outlast the strategic initiative and is something actually separate from it, though we will see the Environmental Goals and Strategies both align and clash with the strategic initiative. As such, we place the Environmental Goals into Table 4.5, and link back to Table 4.4.

Before we do this, we will examine the responses to the questions in the content analysis.

*Question 5*: The question seeks to identify the overall environmental policy or Vision. It is actually quite clear because two of the interviewees quote the new Environmental Vision: (17) Potato Grow promises the earth that it will in no way harm its soil nor its sky nor anything that lives and breathes between the two. One of the interviewees, Abigail, is the company's environmental and energy specialist. So she is driving this initiative.

*Question 6:* Identifies the goals and strategies that will support the Environmental Vision. All interviewees recognise the goal of (18) zero carbon emissions that is supported or achieved by implementing a number of strategies: (19) continue ethical farming practices – no pesticides or chemicals and no GMO, (20) apply environmental practice to clusters to help bring efficiencies, (21) reduce emissions in transport and supply chain, and (22) recruit more farms into the clusters – so Potato Grow can deliver larger orders.

*Question 7:* Asks who will be responsible for the goal and strategies, and how Potato Grow will know it is succeeding. The general view is that Potato Grow, and in particular, Abigail, is driving this environmental initiative but that farmers and their farms will have to do most of the work in terms of ensuring best ethical farming practices. The farmer representative confirms this. It will be our job to explicitly identify responsibilities among the partners. We would then get Potato Grow to validate this. What can be noted from Question 7 is that there are some concrete ways to measure the success of Potato Grow's Environmental Strategies. We will call them tactics because they are targeted actions that are carried out in support of the success of the strategies: (23) capture emissions data through automated meter reading of gas/electric, (24) measure soil acidity and nutrients, and one other that the farmers do that may not have been considered by Potato Grow: (25) maintain the ideal of countryside (maintaining hedgerows and copses for insects and birds, wild flowers for bees, letting fields lie fallow and grow wild). There is also a goal: (26) to reduce fugitive gas emissions (refrigerant leakage when potatoes are stored and transported) and this supports the higher goal of zero carbon emissions.

*Question 8:* Is a key question in which we try to identify the impact of the Environmental Vision on the strategic initiative. As can be seen, there are a number of negative responses – more so than positive. What stands out is the concern that (27) the environmental policy will negatively impact the strategic initiative and put the business at risk. A number of specific conflicts are also mentioned.

Table 4.5      Environmental Strategy

| Business Strategy | Owner/Involves | Impacts/ Conflicts with | Supports/ Aligns to |
|---|---|---|---|
| **VISION** | | | |
| EV: Potato Grow promises the earth that it will in no way harm its soil nor its sky nor anything that lives and breathes between the two. | Potato Grow | Everything | Everything |
| **Goals** | | | |
| EG1: Reduce carbon footprint to zero. | Potato Grow | Farms, farmers, logistics providers, *Initiative Vision* | EVision |
| EG2: Maintain Soil Association certification. | Potato Grow/Soil Association | Farms, farmers | EVision |
| EG3: Achieve ISO16001 certification. | Potato Grow/ISO, Carbon Trust | Potato Grow | EG1 |
| **Strategies** | | | |
| ES1: Implement Energy Management System. | Potato Grow | Potato Grow | EG3 |
| ES2: Examine supply chain and transportation to reduce carbon footprint. | Potato Grow | Logistics providers, *Initiative G2, T2* | EG3 |
| ES3: Continue ethical farming practices – no chemicals, pesticides and GMOs. | Potato Grow, farms, farmers | *Initiative G5* | *Initiative G4, EG2* |
| ES4: Apply best environmental practices to cluster to bring about efficiencies. | Potato Grow, farms, farmers | — | *Initiative T4, EG2* |
| ES5: Recruit ethical farmers/ farms. | Potato Grow | Farms, farmers | *Initiative G4, EG2* |
| **Tactics** | | | |
| ET1: Capture emissions data through automated meter reading of gas and electricity across Potato Grow and farms. | Potato Grow | Potato Grow, farms | ES1 |
| ET2: Capture fugitive emissions data through leakage of refrigerants across Potato Grow. | Potato Grow | Potato Grow | ES1 |
| ET3: Measure soil acidity and nutrients. | Potato Grow, Farmers | Farms | ES3 |
| ET4: Maintain the ideal of countryside. | Farmers | Farms | ES3, ES4 |

## Summary

This chapter has introduced and explained how interviews can be analysed in order to quickly identify recurrent themes, these being goals, strategies and tactics. They could easily be product requirements also. Quick content analysis allows you to then produce a structured table of those goals, strategies and tactics, and identify who or what is responsible for their achievement.

We have discussed the idea of producing graphical models without showing how to do that. Now we ready to address that. Chapter 5 takes you through a step-by-step journey in how to create a goal model from all the information we have gathered and organised thus far.

# Chapter 5
# Strategic Modelling

When you take a look at Table 4.4 it is clear which partners are responsible for what goals, strategies and tactics. So why bother doing something more complex and time consuming such as producing a model? Here's why:

- the model looks cool to customers, making you look an even more valuable asset. Your ability to summarise so much information so succinctly is a powerful ally in persuading your client of your findings;

- good models show inconsistencies and conflicts clearly;

- customers rapidly identify gaps and missing elements;

- a model helps present a consensus view;

- a good model helps stakeholders understand the strategic message and get buy-in;

- the model and table in tandem provide a mechanism for cross checking – once you see the model it becomes much easier to analyse the information. But you need that information in a format that can be readily updated and managed, hence the table.

So how do we build the model? Remember that flowchart where we ask questions to identify specific elements of a strategic model in Figure 3.1? I've reproduced this in this chapter in Figure 5.1 so you don't have to flip back and forth. Those goals, strategies, tactics and partners are important for building a simple yet expressive model of that strategic initiative.

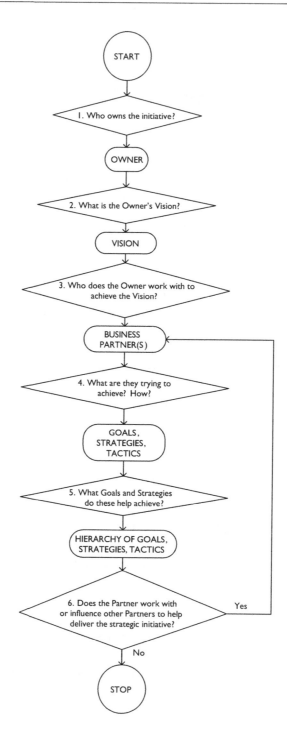

**Figure 5.1    Reproduction of Figure 3.1, strategic initiative interview-modelling flowchart**

These are the steps required in order to draw a strategy model. You simply follow the flowchart and use the data in Table 4.4 to build it. You'll note that I actually have two models. One is of the goals and strategies and the other is focussed on context. I separate the two out to avoid clutter in order to make each model more readable and focussed. I've combined the models in the past but have found clients have struggled with this much information in one picture.

## Goal Modelling

Effectively a goal model is built using the outputs of Steps 2, 4 and 5 from the flowchart in Figure 5.1.

- Step 2: Identify the Vision.

- Step 4: Identify goals, strategies, tactics.

- Step 5: Identify the goal hierarchy.

Given these identifications are already listed in Table 4.4 the hard work is done; it is a straightforward exercise to build the model. Sketch the model out on paper first. This gives you a good feel for the layout and will help you put it into electronic format.

Let us follow the process step-by-step. In Step 2 we will identify the Vision (see Figure 5.2):

**Figure 5.2     Vision goal**

As you can see, we take the Vision statement as identified in the content analysis and in the business strategy Table 4.4 and simply place it into an oval that denotes a goal.

Next, in Step 4 we continue to identify goals, strategies and tactics. Note the shapes are different for goals, strategies and tactics. The shapes are just a mechanism for easier identification. It is up to you what shapes you prefer. Anyway, we can place the goals, strategies and tactics on the page in a sort of linear order. The first three of each are prepared in Figure 5.3 so you can see what is happening:

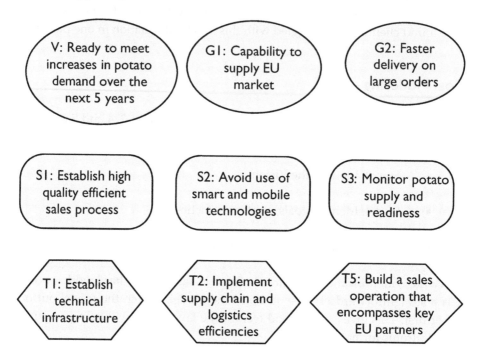

**Figure 5.3     Goals, strategies and tactics**

We now need to place the goals in a hierarchy in order to know what goals contribute to the achievement of others and identify where there are clashes. Recall that a goal is an end-state that we want to achieve and it is supported by a strategy that describes generally how to reach that end-state. A strategy can be supported by a tactic that provides a detail of how to meet the strategy. Goals can contribute to other goals. A softer, more abstract goal can be supported by a more concrete goal, still an end-state but one we can more accurately measure the success of. If we look at Table 4.4 we can see that Goals 1 and 2 directly support the Vision:

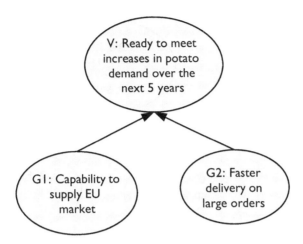

**Figure 5.4    Goal hierarchy snippet**

As you can see, Goals 1 and 2 are now connected via the arrows. The arrows point from Goals 1 and 2 to the Vision Goal to show they contribute to the achievement of the Vision. How do you decide what goal contributes to another? As I mentioned earlier, there is no magic foolproof formula for this. You have to go on what your interviewees and client tell you, and use your own judgement. Remember you are piecing together what might appear to be seemingly disparate goals. This is hard to do but is part and parcel of your role as the expert analyst. But let's get a feel for how you may go about doing this.

Goal 1: *Capability to supply EU market* implies that Potato Grow need to put processes and procedures in place in order to efficiently support the EU market. Given we have identified a strategy of *Establish high-quality efficient sales process* we can reasonably argue that this strategy would in part effectively support the achievement of Goal 1. Hence, we can add Strategy 1 to the goal model showing it supporting Goal 1 via the arrow in Figure 5.5.

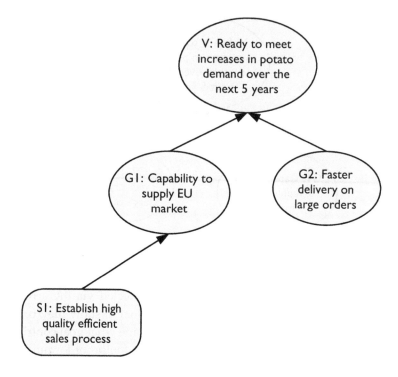

**Figure 5.5     Potato Grow partial goal model with Strategy 1**

If we look at Table 4.4 again we note there is a tactic, T5, *Build a sales operation that encompasses key EU partners*, which should concretely support Strategy 1. You would assume this to be a sensible thing to do hence its inclusion in the model as seen in Figure 5.6.

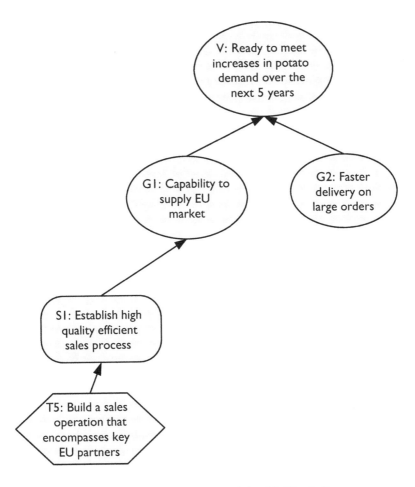

**Figure 5.6    Potato Grow partial goal model with Tactic 5**

Strategy 1 seems to reasonably support Goal 1. It makes sense. But is there anything more? Take a look at Goal 2 *Faster delivery on large orders*. Would that benefit from Strategy 1? A reasonable case can be made that faster delivery is enhanced by a high-quality, efficient sales process. We can say that Strategy 1 actually contributes to both Goals 1 and 2 though in different ways. Here's where you may want to re-read the wording of Strategy 1. The first word says 'Establish'. In order to be capable of supplying the EU market (Goal 1), Potato Grow must first establish a high-quality efficient sales process (Strategy 1). In order for Potato Grow to ensure faster delivery on large orders (Goal 2), a high-quality and efficient sales process should have been established (S1). It is hard to argue against this being a valid statement. Figure 5.7 shows now that Strategy 1 contributes also to Goal 2. You will also see Strategy 2, *Avoid use of smart and mobile technologies,* supporting the achievement of Goals 1 and 2.

We have explained earlier that more and more scientists are recognising the harmful impact of microwave radiation on the nature kingdom, and this is something directly contrary to the Environmental Strategy of the company. An interesting thing about this strategy is that it does not tell what to do, rather what not to do. This is because any alternative, provided it is non-harming, will do.

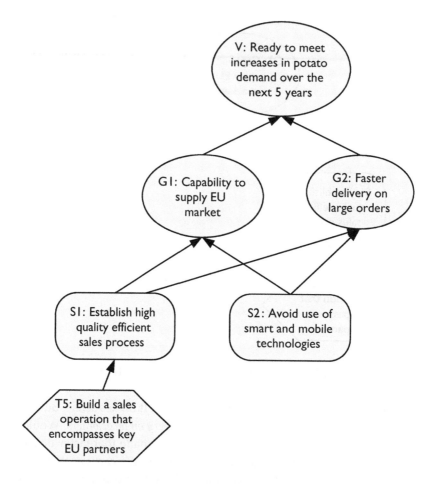

**Figure 5.7    Partial goal model with Strategy 2 and further contribution link for Strategy 1**

To reiterate the point, strategic planning is about taking considered chances as much as joining the dots. But those chances need to be well thought out to proceed at all. Visibility in the plan provides the first step in that thought process.

If we take a look back at Table 4.4, we can add a further goal, G3, to the model and so get the following goal model chunk in Figure 5.8:

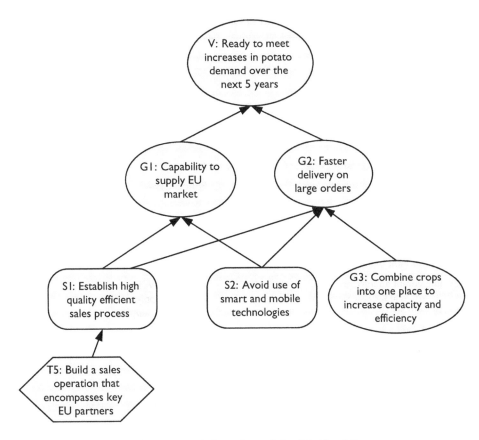

**Figure 5.8    Potato Grow partial goal model with Goal 3**

Goal 3, *Combine crops in one place to increase capacity and efficiency* would naturally contribute to G2. But let's think about G3 more closely. Is it really an end-state to *combine crops in one place*? That is, is this goal really a goal? No, it sounds like more of a strategy because it is an action thing, a doing thing and doing it on a large scale. But what of the other half of the statement: *to increase capacity and efficiency*? This seems fairly abstract to me so would qualify as a goal. To make it less abstract, we will add context so it now reads, *Increase capacity and efficiency of farms*. So we may need to split G3 in two: G3 plus a supporting strategy. This means we need to revise Table 4.4. It now looks like Table 5.1.

**Table 5.1      Business strategy table: Potato Grow strategic
initiative revised**

| Business Strategy | Main Partner | Supporting Partners | Helps Achieve |
|---|---|---|---|
| **VISION** | | | |
| V: Ready to meet increases in potato demand over the next five years. | Potato Grow | — | — |
| **Goals** | | | |
| G1: Capability to supply EU market. | Potato Grow | EU market | V |
| G2: Faster delivery on large orders. | Potato Grow | Customers | V |
| G3: Increase capacity and efficiency of farms. | Farms | Potato Grow | G1, G2 |
| G4: Ensure farmers get a good deal. | Potato Grow | Farmer | V |
| G5: Increase potato crop capacity by 200 per cent within 12 months. | Potato Grow | Farms | G3 |
| G6: Implement an infrastructure within two years; applications by end of year 3. | IT dept | Potato Grow, farms, logistics, supply chain, sales, supplier relations | G3 |
| G7: Produce a contract to guarantee relationships between farmers and Potato Grow remain good. | Potato Grow | Farmers | G4 |
| G8: Reduce potato quality assessments by two days. | Farms | Potato Grow | G3 |
| **Strategies** | | | |
| S1: Establish high-quality efficient sales process. | Sales | Customers, EU market | G1, G2 |
| S2: Avoid use of smart and mobile technologies. | IT dept | Potato Grow | G1, G2 |
| S3: Monitor potato supply and readiness. | IT dept | Farms, sales, logistic providers | G3 |
| S4: Guarantee business/sustainable income. | Potato Grow | Farmer | G4 |
| S5: Streamline crop quantity assessment. | Potato Grow | Farms | G8 |
| S6: Combine crops in one place. | Potato Grow | Farms | G5 |
| **Tactics** | | | |
| T1: Establish technical infrastructure. | IT dept | Farms, sales, logistic providers | S3 |

| Business Strategy | Main Partner | Supporting Partners | Helps Achieve |
| --- | --- | --- | --- |
| T2: Implement supply chain and logistics efficiencies. | Supply chain | Logistics providers, customers | S3 |
| T3: Assess current process for entire potato lifecycle. | IT dept | Potato Grow, farms, logistics, supply chain, sales, supplier relations | G6 |
| T4: Plan phased change to not disrupt current business. | Potato Grow | Farms | S4 |
| T5: Build a sales operation that encompasses key EU partners. | Sales | EU market, customers | S1 |

As can be seen in the table, there is a new Strategy, S6, *Combine crops in one place* which implies that cluster farms are the way to go. Strategy 6 contributes to the achievement of Goal 5. We might argue that S6 should contribute to both G3 and G5. In an indirect way, it does. G5 is a concrete goal in that it is something we can precisely measure. The Strategy S6 will explicitly help in measuring the success of G5. This combined with G6 and G8, can also be measured, and is well supported and/or implemented by Tactic T3 and Strategy S5 respectively will give an overall better indication of the success of G3. We are, to use an analogy, closely assessing the behaviour of children in an attempt to understand the children's parent. So it makes more sense to have strategies and tactics to support our assessment of the children so we at least know we have some accurate data and we can then more effectively judge the parent. The result of the splitting of G3 (see Figure 5.8 for original) and addition of Goals G6 and G8 with supporting strategies and tactic is shown in Figure 5.9.

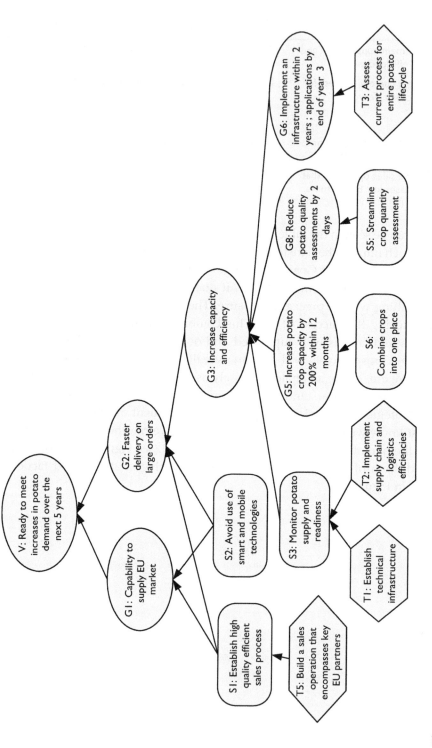

Figure 5.9    Revised goal model after dividing Goal 3

The remaining goals that have not been addressed are something of a tangent but nonetheless critical to the success of Potato Grow's initiative. These goals revolve around the relationship with the farmers. Goal 4 states that *farmers should get a good deal*. This is so important to Potato Grow that this goal contributes directly to the Vision Goal. Without happy farmers, Potato Grow's initiative is simply going to fail. To help achieve that goal, a Strategy, S4, *guarantee business/sustainable income* needs to be implemented. To help in implementing this strategy we have identified one tactic, T4, *Plan phased change to not disrupt current business*. This makes good sense. Big bang changes rarely work and in the world of farming would be virtually impossible simply because nature dances to its own tune.

If you take a look at Goal 7, which contributes to the achievement of G4, *Produce a contract to guarantee relationships between farmers and Potato Grow remain good* you might wonder if this is really a goal. It seems more tactical. Perhaps it is. There is a good reason, though, to keep this as a goal. First, this is a short-term target and as such qualifies as a goal. We haven't placed a time frame on it but we imagine it is quite important to get right sooner rather than later given all the other targets and pressures on Potato Grow. Second, this is not something that is ongoing; in other words, we should not be rewriting our standard boilerplate contracts every other week. There may be a degree of variation because of size of farm or location or farming method, but what Potato Grow will offer farmers should be standard. There's no point offering a different deal to each farm because farmers talk and this is a sure fire way to negate Goal 4: if that farmer is getting 'this' deal, why can't I? So again, as it is not a long operational or tactical activity, I suggest we leave G7 as a goal. Figure 5.10 shows the complete Potato Grow strategic initiative goal model.

Please note, the goal model is not complete – although I just said it was. We have only shown goals that we have captured and presented earlier in this book. If we have interviewed another 10 stakeholders we may well have a whole lot more goals to deal with.

What else is missing? What about those Environmental Goals and Strategies that Potato Grow are also taking on board as part of their future? Table 4.5 showed us the Environmental Goals, strategies and tactics. We can take the same approach as just described in producing the Environmental Goal Model.

If we went through the same process as we have above for creating the strategic initiative goal model we would end up with an Environmental Goal Model something akin to that shown in Figure 5.11.

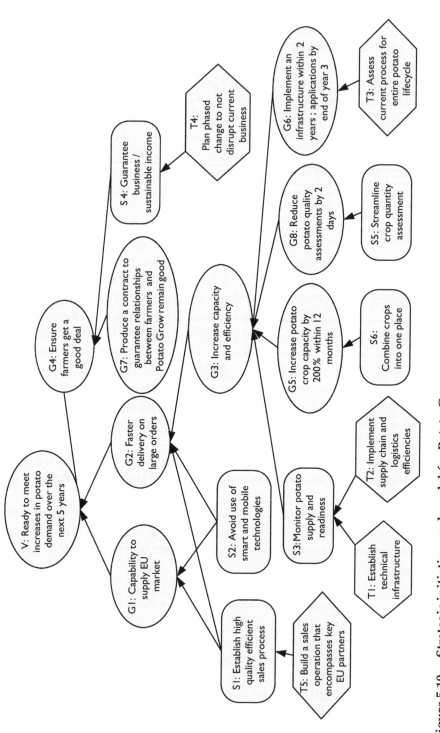

**Figure 5.10   Strategic initiative goal model for Potato Grow**

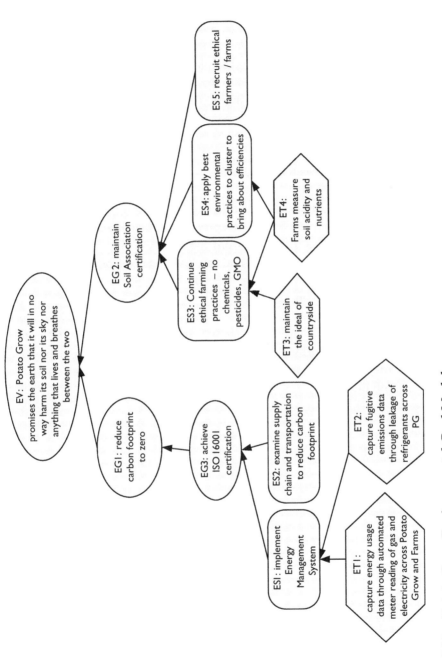

Figure 5.11   Potato Grow Environmental Goal Model

There is no difference in the notation or approach to developing and reading the Environmental Goal Model because in our eyes all goals are goals. To distinguish, an 'E' has been added before the V, G, S, T. So the Environmental Model looks interesting enough as it is; however, it is to some extent isolated because it there is no direct connection to the Strategic Goal Model as seen in Figure 5.10 above. This is easily resolved by placing Figure 5.11 next to Figure 5.10, or the Strategic Goal Model next to the Environmental Goal Model, as see in Figure 5.12. By doing this we are bringing together a connection between the models in the form of dependencies or conflicts. These are shown in Figure 5.12 and explained here:

- Conflict between G5 and ES3:

    There is a high risk of conflict because the time frame set for the achievement of G5 is short; corners may be cut and this could lead to a loss of certification from the Soil Association. When time is short, quality is reduced and carelessness is introduced.

- Impact between T2 and ES2:

    T2 supply chain efficiencies will probably impact the ES2 reduce carbon footprint goal; we don't know if this will be a positive, negative or neutral impact yet. There is a chance this will impact on EG1 also.

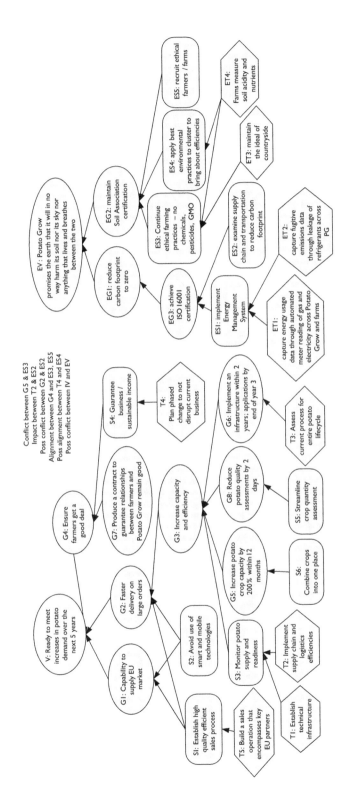

**Figure 5.12** Side-by-side strategic initiative and Environmental Goal Models with notes on potential touch points

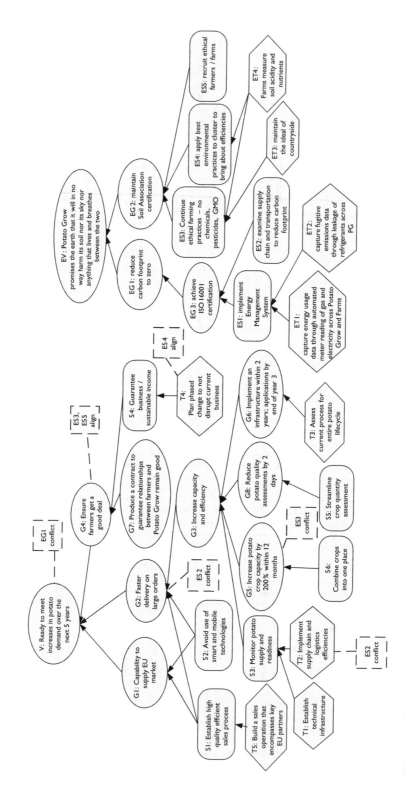

Figure 5.13    Integrated initiative and Environmental Goal Model via conflicts and alignment notes

Figure 5.13 presents a top-down model of strategies, goals and tactics and is a powerful way to present a business strategy model. It's built top-down, rather than for instance left-to-right, in order to better show what matters most. In our thinking, it's the more abstract statements such as the Vision and Goals 1, 2 and 4 that are considered the most significant. Strategies are implemented to support the achievement of goals. Strategies tend to be companywide or heavily impact the customer. Tactics make up the achievement of a strategy and are more focussed on individual departments or a subset of departments. Tactics can also achieve lower level, more concrete goals.

A model is an excellent thing but takes more effort, so what if you were to stick with only Table 5.1? You would miss out on the sense of hierarchy and structure that a table simply cannot give you. The goal alignment and dependency becomes clear the instant you look at Figure 5.13. Why does this matter? When a manager is given the responsibility to implement Tactic 3 and he begins to wonder where this tactic fits in the bigger picture then by taking a quick look at this figure, it becomes clear how important this tactic really is. Your client can also validate your findings far more readily than having to read through a 200-page, text-laden, stodgy report. In one picture the client can now reason about the choice of strategies and the risks of failing to deliver on tactical or operational activities.

But there's something missing. Figure 5.13 is powerful at reflecting about goals and putting them in a hierarchy but does little to address responsibilities. Who or what is responsible for the achievement of those goals?

## Context Modelling

We need to not only identify but also create a strategic partner model. This is constructed using the outputs of Steps 1, 3 and 6 in the flowchart in Figure 5.1.

- Step 1: Identify the initiative owner.

- Step 3: Identify the main partners (which often also includes the initiative owner).

- Step 6: Identify other partners the main partners work with to achieve the Vision.

The model then associates those goals, strategies and tactics described above to the partners. It's easy to do because we have already tabulated the relationships in Tables 5.1 and 4.5 (Environmental Goals/partners). We just use those tables to create the partner context models because they show us the main artner and supporting partners in the columns of the tables.

So let's begin with the first step: identify and model the initiative owner, and include the identifiers of Vision and Environmental Vision in Figure 5.14:

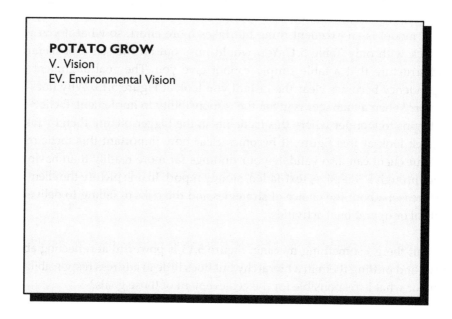

**POTATO GROW**
V. Vision
EV. Environmental Vision

**Figure 5.14     Initiative owner, Vision and Environmental Vision**

All we have done is use a simple box. For all the context entities: partners, we just use a box and their name. Some we place inside Potato Grow because they are departments within it. Others we will place outside because they are not part of the internal operations of Potato Grow.

Figure 5.15 shows the Potato Grow in terms of goal ownership and responsibilities for Goals G1 to G5 and Goals G7 and G8, only showing external partners:

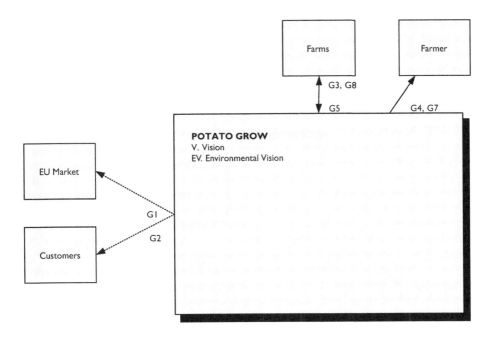

**Figure 5.15    Potato Grow and some external partners**

As can be seen, the model is rather simple but that is all we need. Potato Grow has four external partners in Figure 5.15, customers, EU market, farms and farmers. The arrows indicate direction of responsibility. Potato Grow is responsible for G1 and G2 (Capability to supply EU market; faster delivery on large orders); that is why the goal label is placed next to Potato Grow rather than the partners. We see that Potato Grow has the responsibility of achieving Goals G4 and G7 for the farmer. Note the double-headed arrow between Potato Grow and the partner farms. Here we see a two-way flow. The arrow heads effectively just reinforce the message of how to read goal responsibility. The farms are actually responsible for Goals 3 and 8 because although they are part of Potato Grow's strategy, Potato Grow itself cannot achieve them. It needs farms to do this. But Potato Grow should ensure G5 for the farms.

The next step is to include the internal partners involved in achieving the goals. This is shown in Figure 5.16.

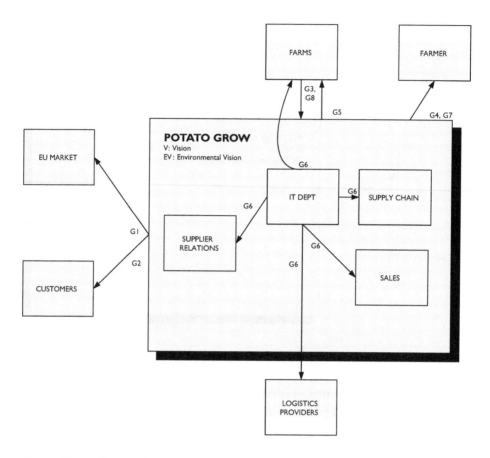

**Figure 5.16    Potato Grow, partners (internal and external) and goals**

As can be seen, Figure 5.16 shows the IT department is responsible internally for delivering Goal G6 (Implement an infrastructure within two years; applications by end of year 3) to the departments of supplier relations, supply chain and sales. The IT department is also responsible for achieving G6 for the farms. Note a new external partner, logistics, is also identified as part of the context of G6 and added to the figure. We can see that Goal G6 is pretty significant to the success of this initiative.

We can add in the strategies into the figure in the same way as we have the goals. This is shown in Figure 5.17.

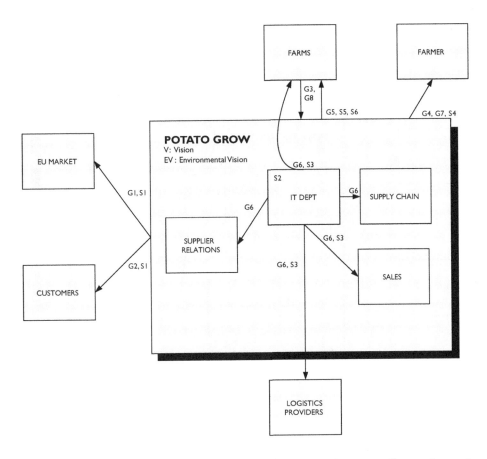

**Figure 5.17** **Potato Grow, partners (internal and external), goals and strategies**

One thing to note in Figure 5.17 is S2 (use of smart and mobile technologies) is within the IT department box. The reason to put it here is because the IT department is responsible for rolling this out across all of Potato Grow including all of its various departments. It is akin to the Vision statement for Potato Grow that effectively holds true for the whole company, or at least all those within Potato Grow participating in this strategic initiative. The next step is to add the tactics as listed in Table 5.1 to the model, as can be seen in Figure 5.18.

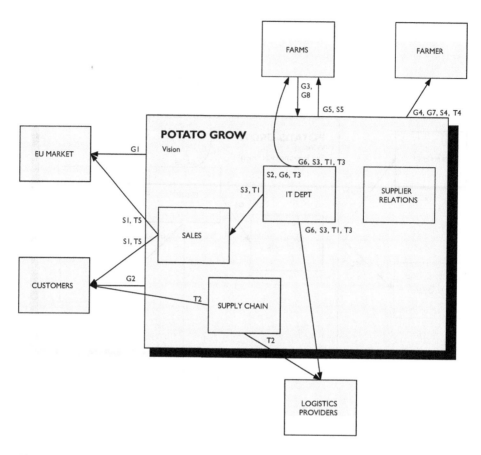

**Figure 5.18    Potato Grow, partners (internal and external), goals, strategies and tactics**

As can be seen, the model has been reorganised to reposition internal partners sales and supply chain in order to have more direct access to external entities. The model can quickly become very busy and this is a good reason for drawing one. If you want to quickly and accurately keep track of context and goals then this is a good start. As soon as any changes appear, then you may even model them first before updating the tables in order to keep a more clear mental and visual track of those changes.

What about those Environmental Goals and Strategies listed in Table 4.5? Well, perhaps the best place to begin understanding where this fits or conflicts with our *initiative* context partner model is to build a separate context model for Environmental Goals, Strategies and Tactics. The same principles are followed as above and the resultant context model is shown in Figure 5.19. As can be seen, we have new partners, Soil Association and the ISO/Carbon Trust.

All that remains from the initiative context are the farms, farmers and logistics providers. We also have a new link between the farmers and farms. We may well have drawn the farmer as *within* a farm as we did with Potato Grow and its departments as seen above. But I chose not to do this because I felt from the case, from the interviews, that there was enough justification to keep them separate in the model. This is down to personal choice. It really wouldn't matter if you chose a different way to do this so long as you are consistent and clear in your model and explanations.

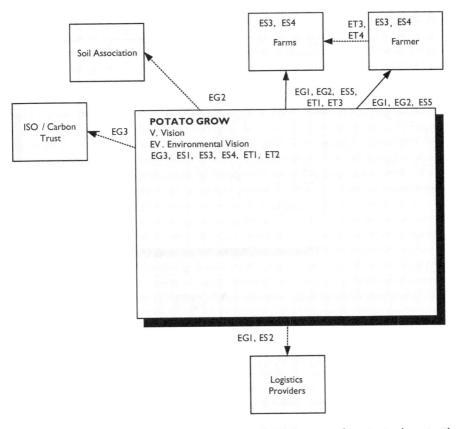

**Figure 5.19 Potato Grow Environmental Vision, goals, strategies, tactics and partners**

We now have two context models in the same way we had two goal models as shown in Figure 5.13. What can we do from here? We could overlay one against the other or combine the two. We would see quite a big model and quite a messy model too. But that is often the way it goes in modelling. To hide the mess or complexity, or as the saying goes, to abstract away the complexity, is to leave something that may not have enough depth to mean anything. So below we have Figure 5.20, which is a combination of both models. I have coloured the environmental partners if not already in the initiative model in 5.18 and the Environmental Goal identifiers differently so they stand out.

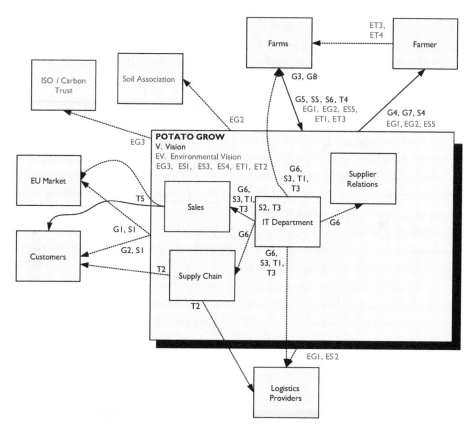

**Figure 5.20** **Potato Grow initiative and Environmental Vision, goals, strategies, tactics and partners**

What isn't represented are the conflicting goals here. But that is ably captured in both the goal models and the tables so it isn't entirely necessary to muddle the diagram further just here. Saying that, if you wanted to add the explicit conflicts, you might either put the table directly below the model to show or to annotate Figure 5.20 with the further information. Both are up to you. There's nothing wrong with either, or just leaving it at that.

## Summary

This chapter has been about modelling goals and context. The key point of this is to provide a viewpoint rarely seen in strategy and IT documentation, a picture of the goal – business context. It provides an interesting and relatively straightforward way to do analysis beyond tables and spreadsheets. Often requirements documents are extended tables or spreadsheets. There's often a lot of design notation such as how software may work, and there are business process models and even business models that are relatively graphical. You can find a lot of literature in the academic world on goal modelling that is pretty dense and complex to follow. I should know as I co-wrote a few of those papers! But if you need something rapid but expressive, the above will be of assistance to you. Just one last note: you will no doubt find many different modelling notations on both goal and context modelling and some of it will look very similar to the above. If that is the case then I state clearly now those alternatives are probably more complete and rigorous to what is above. I have used the above in cases just to produce quick models. If there were a software tool to make it even quicker then so much the better. I have found that understanding the models varies from 'crystal clear' to 'no idea'. So it is up to you to educate your clients. All I can say is keep it really simple and clear. Yet do not abstract the complexity out of the problem. There is a risk of over-simplifying to the point of making it too simple to be of value. As Einstein once said, 'Make it simple, but not too simple.'

Now you have your models, how do you present what you have back to your client?

# Chapter 6

# Presenting Your Work

*I've only got 15 minutes to convince the CEO so presenting me a 200-page document doesn't do anything to help.*
*A senior executive commenting on consultants*
*who put the kitchen sink into their report.*

It's one thing to get all the information you need out your interviews and even to do the analysis. The difficult part is to present your findings in a convincing manner. It's the final report, the presentation and summaries you provide your client that make the difference. You have to report back what you found in a coherent and well-presented way. You have to not only make the final presentation look professional but your recommendations have to be something your client wants to swallow.

If your remit is to document a strategy for implementing a new product, you need to make it convincing. If you're a BA who has to produce a requirements document, you'd better make sure it doesn't contain inconsistencies. Let's face it, if you're a contractor who has been hired to produce a report or document or presentation and/or give recommendations about anything, then you will need to make a good job of it.

There are a number of ways you can provide feedback and present your work. To keep things simple, in order to convince the CEO and your client, here's a list of what this chapter will cover:

- the one-page interviewee summary;

- getting feedback on the models;

- the interim report;

- the final report;

- making the executive pitch: slides and speech;

- presenting to the masses.

## One-Page Summary

The purpose of the one-page summary is four-fold.

1.   To get interviewees to validate the findings from their interview.

2.   To manage your own thoughts and to place the findings within the context of the engagement. It's important to quickly produce summaries of the key points in an interview for you and your team.

3.   Your client is bound to ask you how things are going and what you have found out so far. So it makes sense for you to effectively keep notes of the key points. If you can reel off a few of these to your client, he should be fairly impressed.

4.   Each one-pager can be inserted into the final, and interim, report more or less as is. This means you are effectively putting the final report together as you conduct your analysis and validation.

### DOS AND DON'TS OF THE ONE-PAGER

- Do send a one-page summary of key points made by the interviewee if you have been asked and have been given approval to send feedback. If you absolutely must use a quotation from the interview, you *absolutely must* get permission from the interviewee, even if the perpetrator of the quotation remains anonymous in the report and presentation.

- Don't expect interviewees to sign anything that might commit them to what has been written on paper unless it is of absolutely no consequence to them and has absolutely no impact on their current job. And if this is the case, why interview them in the first place? This is what is euphemistically called the CYA principle: Cover Your Arse. If you don't know what this means, you'll soon find out.

- Don't send any models you've produced from the interviews – no one will understand them – unless the interviewee explicitly asked to see a model because he knew you were going to produce one. And then you'll have to prepare a 'how to read this model' document to accompany it.

- This next point may seem to be obvious but people like me make this mistake: Don't forget to provide a summary, and don't present an entire word-for-word transcript of an interview back to the interviewee for validation. Every interview transcript will be filled with babble, confusion and chaos as an interviewee formulates coherent responses to your questions. Failing to send a severely edited transcription – *one-page only* – to the interviewee is not good for the health as I found out, especially if the interviewee is a senior manager or executive.

## SCENARIO: BE CAREFUL WHAT YOU SEND TO YOUR CLIENT FOR REVIEW

I once made this mistake on an engagement with a large government agency. I had interviewed a number of very senior managers and was in the process of writing up transcripts of recordings. I inadvertently sent one of the most senior managers the entire unadulterated transcription for validation. I was delighted to see her reply email in my inbox the same day. When I read the email, the smile was wiped from my face. She was politely furious. I had to apologise both via email and over the phone. Quite rightly, given the significance of the project under discussion, she was very annoyed and was probably wondering what kind of idiot I was because she was worried about how her opinion and herself might be represented to her managers and peers. I sent her the one-pager, with quotes, and bullet points only, post haste. She immediately validated it and agreed I could use this summary in my report. But she remained cold towards me for the remainder of the project and this was no doubt a contributory factor to why we didn't get her company's business afterwards as we thought we would.

Note: I have provided the complete report only rather than take pieces out of it for the one-pager and interim reports. It is straightforward to decide what to put into the one-pager and interim report so I leave this to the reader.

## WHAT'S IN THE ONE-PAGER?

Here's a list of things I would include:

- interviewee name and role, date of interview;

- context for interview (a brief statement);

- quotations – only if permission granted from the interviewee (and your client to put the quote into the final report);

- key points made in interview (these should reflect the overriding objective and specific interview objectives);

- your contact details.

That's it. In the covering email, state what you plan to do with the feedback. And keep the document to one page; I can't say this enough.

You have probably realised that the content analysis in Chapter 4 can be employed to help in providing the summarised bullet points for the one-pager. This means you probably don't have to trawl through the interview transcript except to find a quote, if you are willing to use quotes at all. I may seem a little over cautious when it comes to quotes. There's a reason for this. Quotes have a habit of being used out of context and in the case of a review or in reference to a controversial point such as an unpopular strategy, the quote can be used as a weapon against the responsible individual. This is a shame because you may only ever get to use highly positive quotes ('Yes' men quotes) or bland ones (in which case why bother?). Anonymity helps but most people in organisations who work together can recognise the style and tone of a colleague's statement and can and do throw mud even if it is at the wrong target. You're not there to cause problems, but to remedy them, making the world a better place in the process. So that's why I would be cautious about quotes no matter how profound they can be.

A one-pager almost writes itself, but not quite. As you can see, it's relatively straightforward to put these together in order to facilitate feedback and for later report writing. This is all you need to do for the one-pager. A note of caution: please keep this to only one page even if you think each and every comment made in the interview is of paramount significance. The reasons are: (1) if you add every point that is key you'll end up presenting an almost entire transcript;

and (2) you want really quick feedback so keep it short. The interviewee will tell you if you have missed something she deemed to be of higher significance than your findings. If you get a comment like this, add it to your findings even if you find it surprising the interviewee thought the point significant. She has far more insight than you, remember. If you really have doubts, find out why the interviewee thinks it is important and ask a couple of other interviewees of their opinion of the point. Don't say, 'Sheila thinks "x" matters. Is she barking up the wrong tree?' Be a bit more subtle than that. And don't name interviewees when talking to others, except your client and only if agreed in advance that naming an interviewee won't get that interviewee into trouble.

## Feedback on Models

I've mentioned that it isn't a good idea to email interviewees any models you've put together such as the strategic goal and partner models, or any others you might have done. The reason for this is that the interviewee will need an explanation of that model from you. Not so much about the text in the boxes but the boxes themselves and the connections between them.

So maybe you shouldn't get feedback on the models? No, I'm not saying that. You will have to get feedback because modelling is an important part of your analysis and dissemination of results. Also, the models should impress the interviewees provided the models are not too simplistic. You will need to put both models side-by-side to give the most complete picture.

The best way to get feedback is to print the models on a good-sized paper so that they are easy to read. Sit down with the interviewee and walk through the model. Explain what the boxes mean. Be prepared to give the interviewee carte blanche to scrawl on the paper making changes as he sees fit. For each change ask 'why?' I would even record the feedback session and take copious notes.

Do you show the final models you have from the combination of interviews done or do you just present the single interviewee's model? I would always go for the combined model on the grounds that: (1) the single model will almost always be only a fragment; and (2) you can validate your other findings at the same time.

I wouldn't spend much more than 20 minutes getting this feedback. If it takes a lot longer it is either because the model is too complicated to understand or you can't explain it well enough or the interviewee/client is red-pen-happy making endless amendments. If you find yourself in the first two situations then you need to work on your presentation and explanatory skills. I would recommend you don't use a model in these circumstances. If you're in the last situation, then there are two reasons for this: (1) you've got the entire model wrong and your take on the situation is miles out; or (2) you're on the right track but perhaps haven't pitched at the right level of abstraction or have missed something fundamental. In both cases take careful note of the extended feedback. Later check this feedback with others to make sure it makes sense.

## KEY VALIDATION QUESTIONS TO ASK ABOUT THE STRATEGIC GOAL MODEL

When presenting a Strategic Goal Model for feedback you need to find out the following:

- Correct goals: are there any goals/strategies/tactics missing or surplus to requirements? Is the wording of those goals/strategies/tactics more or less reasonable?

- Hierarchy links: are the goals, strategies and tactics structured in the right way? Does the goal to sub-goal hierarchy appear correct?

- Hidden dependencies: what links are missing?

## KEY VALIDATION QUESTIONS TO ASK ABOUT THE STRATEGIC PARTNER MODEL

When presenting a strategic partner model for feedback you need to find out the following:

- Are all partners correctly labelled?

- Are any partners missing/superfluous?

- Is the partner-to-partner structure correct?

- Do the positioning of goals, strategies and tactics make sense?

## The Interim Report

You will be expected to present an ongoing report at some point during your engagement that shows your paymasters you're on the right track, have discovered some wonderful things and are on the verge of discovering more. In other words, the role of the interim report for the client is to convince herself or himself that hiring you was a good idea. As an internal BA, you ought to consider presenting an interim report to your business or project manager because the report should inform that manager of how the project is progressing.

The interim report is also an opportunity for you to play with the presentation format. But beware whichever one you choose now should be used again in the final report, unless your client tells you otherwise. You should ask because you want to make sure you're providing the best service. Find out what resonates best with your clients and then stick to that format, provided it is appropriate for the job. If you're stuck with a company's template and are not happy with it (most of it is irrelevant and/or it looks ugly structurally), change the template or ignore it.

The contents of a report should be short, sharp and strong. Short: cut out all repetition, flowery language and unnecessary prelude. Sharp: all points should be on target; if you can't think of something sharp to put, don't put it. Strong: all points must be bold and defendable. Weak statements will get shredded by your client and ignored by the people who are supposed to take note of your findings. What if you find a poor project manager is a problem point you wish to make? But how to do that? Is it poor project management throughout? Are there specific activities not done? Do the managers lack certain key qualities? It's no good telling someone they are bad and that they should be better. Everyone knows this but they all disagree with you because you can't pinpoint the specific activity or characteristic that is missing and tell them how to fix it.

The basic components of an interim report are the same as those of your final report. The key points to include are the following:

- the word DRAFT;

- very brief 'Background';

- context of the engagement;

- scope of report;

- key findings in brief;

- detailed findings of note;

- that word DRAFT, again.

You can add any models and/or tables. I tend to avoid these for now because your results are going to change as you progress through the project. But this is a personal preference – I don't want to put too much work on my plate when I am only halfway through the interviews. If your client or manager is keen to see something different then show the models that you have for now. Let's look at each point in more detail.

## THE WORD DRAFT

Hopefully whatever you present to your client or manager will be used or socialised in some shape or form. This is both positive and risky for you. It's positive because this means your work is valued and this ought to give you a sense of achievement and if all goes well, and the opportunity is there, further work. There are risks: (1) your interim findings are acted upon before you discover the findings are wrong; (2) your findings are ignored completely by everyone either because they are banal or wrong or right; (3) your findings are used against you – in other words, the findings are used as ammunition to sabotage your work because the findings threaten someone's agenda.

Hence, using the DRAFT word liberally not just in the document but also in your cover email, assuming you mail it, helps you if things start to go bad.

## VERY BRIEF 'BACKGROUND'

If you write a five-page background section, you'll get the report thrown back in your face. Aim for half a side only. I would make this part of the report a bulleted list, headed by, 'The purpose of this report is...'

- to find out something ...

- for such and such people ...

- to make recommendations for improvement/change.

Effectively, this is a list. That's all you need.

## CONTEXT OF THE ENGAGEMENT

This is a brief paragraph that outlines the background for the project or engagement with you and specifically states what your role is as agreed with your client. In other words, this is an opportunity to scope the boundary of your engagement.

## SCOPE OF THE REPORT

Again, this is a brief statement where you have the chance to limit any potential damage. For instance, if you've interviewed five people in a department of 200, now is the time to state the findings are not statistically representative of the department. The trick, though, is not to downplay the significance of the findings to the point of trivia. You need a comeback, such as, 'although only five people were interviewed and the findings reflect their opinions alone, these five are the only customer-facing staff in the department and speak with authority of that subject.'

## KEY FINDINGS IN BRIEF

This is the at-a-glance-summary section. You just list the key points related to key areas here:

- Key area 1

  - Point 1
  - Point 2
  - ...

- Key area 2

  - Point 1
  - Point 2
  - ...

... and so on.

Make sure the key points and each sub-point are strong statements. This is going to be the most read and used section of your report.

## DETAILED FINDINGS

If you feel the need to add more detail to a particular point or interview, this is the place to do it. This elaboration should take the same structure as your one-page summaries. Reuse is golden. Add more description if needed but keep it to a few sentences. No one wants to, or will, read a long essay justifying one point.

## THAT WORD DRAFT, AGAIN

This is the only repetition I recommend; just make sure it is clear the report is a Draft version.

Don't forget: use headed paper or a company template to present the interim findings. Even though this is 'casual over coffee' feedback, you still high-quality standards either as an independent consultant, representing a larger organisation or as an internal BA or as a researcher or student in a university.

### Email feedback

Sometimes you'll present interim findings in an email. Often this is good enough if your relationship with your client is a long and trusting one. You should be careful to structure the email. I tend to use bullet points only. You can follow a similar format to above except I would not worry about the final section on detailed findings. The last thing people want is to receive a long-winded email. It just won't get read. I'd still label the findings in the email as draft for discussion purposes.

## The Final Report

The final report you deliver is an extension of the interim report. There are a few things you need to add to transition from partial to complete. Naturally, you'll need more material. You'll also add more context and structure.

I am always surprised at how much information gets into a final report. I aim to keep the report as short, sharp and strong as possible. Delivering on sharp and strong is less difficult than keeping it short. Even my shortest engagements or most straightforward ones have ended with a 30 plus-page report, including all appendices and models. Every time I get to that report I think about my client's 15 minutes with the CEO and ask two questions:

(1) Is my message loud, clear and understood in 15 minutes? (2) Can my client reiterate that message in less than 15 minutes to her management and colleagues?

The structure of the final report should[1] look something like this:

- the word DRAFT;

- very brief 'Background';

- context;

- scope of report;

- interviewee list;

- structure of the report/how to read the report;

- key findings in brief;

- detailed findings (there may be several sub-sections that will reflect your context);

- appendices;

- that word DRAFT, again.

I won't go over the repeated points again – take a look above. Below are some words on the new entries to the document.

## INTERVIEWEE LIST

I always recommend you list the names of the people you interviewed and their roles. I'd structure the list into different departments or divisions as well. This helps you client interpret the coverage you've had across the organisation. It also shows any bias, for instance in a heavily one-sided list where 25 operational staff were interviewed about introducing changes to working practices in comparison to three managers. If you've got a bias like this, warn

---

1   I use the word 'should' because you will alter the structure to meet your specific context. The list provided is just a recommendation.

the client in advance. You might have to redress the balance before moving on to the final report. Finally, the list will make it clear to the client who you missed whom she thought important to interview, and whom you added that wasn't on the list originally.

## STRUCTURE OF THE REPORT/HOW TO READ THE REPORT

This is a small section that provides the reader with a 'map' of the report. It's straightforward. You summarise each section context, not content. In other words, you will state that section 3, for example, will explore the anticipated effects of reorganising the IT department in light of the merger proposal with stakeholder quotes, key concerns and key identifiable risks. You don't provide any content on the quotes, concerns or risks here.

## APPENDICES

The appendices will contain data tables such as a strategy initiative table and any other material you consider useful as supporting evidence to justify your case. You may include any models here as well or you might keep them in the main part of the report in the 'Detailed Findings' section.

## EXAMPLE FINAL REPORT

The following example report is not full in the sense that taking over 30 pages does nothing for you reading this book; below are example excerpts of the key points:

## Potato Grow Ltd Strategic Initiative DRAFT Final Report

DRAFT for discussion 28 April 2015

Author: Karl Cox

## BACKGROUND

The purpose of this report is to:

- establish a shared understand of Potato Grow's strategic initiative;

- identify any conflicts or potential problems, especially the Environmental Vision and Strategy;

- recommend any changes to the plan and to resolve conflicts and/or potential problems.

## CONTEXT

A medium-sized organisation, Potato Grow Ltd, manages the supply of potatoes to a leading producer of frozen potato products such as oven chips. Potato Grow decided to expand its footprint into the potato patch to become a major player in the potato supply sector. Potato Grow takes its impact on the environment very seriously and only works with organic farms who do not use pesticides of any kind or GMOs, both of which cause cancer and are designed to kill life. A critical goal for Potato Grow is to make sure its farming practices remain ethical and organic with a longer-term goal of reducing its carbon footprint to zero.

## SCOPE OF THE REPORT

This draft final report reflects the thoughts and opinions of all senior executives and a sample of representative operational staff and associates who are ultimately responsible for implementing the plan (10 interviews). The report reflects the opinions of these stakeholders only.

## INTERVIEWEE LIST

Executive:

- Ed, CEO Potato Grow Ltd

- Joe, Supply Chain Director, Strategic Initiative Lead

- Peter, Director Sales

- Bill, Director Supplier Relations

- Warren, Chief Information Officer

- Abigail, Environmental Director

- ...

Operational Staff and Associates:

- Shannon, Logistics and Supply Chain manager

- Daniel, Cluster Potato Farmer Representative

- William, Farmer

- ...

## STRUCTURE OF THE REPORT

The report has the following structure.

Section 1 presents Key Findings in Brief for the Potato Grow strategic initiative: strategies, potential conflicts or issues and opportunities.

Section 2 presents a breakdown and description of Potato Grow's:

- strategic initiative;

- feedback from stakeholders;

- strategic goals and business partners models.

Section 3 explores and explains:

- conflicts identified in the model;

- opportunities for resolving them.

The Appendix lists:

- supporting data for the models presented in section 2;

- supporting evidence;

- 'how to read the models'.

## SECTION 1: KEY FINDINGS IN BRIEF

- Imperative to bring change into the organisation within the next five years (unanimous agreement among executive team).

- Current business structure failing – missing business opportunities because of process and capacity weaknesses (90 per cent agreement on failure of business structure; disagreement on reasons and remedies).

- Key strategy of clustering potato farms.

- Monitoring of supply and availability seen as critical.

- 12-month capacity increase target of 200 per cent doubtful given no infrastructure in place to support this.

- No notion of how this target aligns with the five-year Vision.

- No medium targets set beyond 12 months – where does Potato Grow go from here?

- No risk identification if target not met 100 per cent at 12 months or five years: what happens to Potato Grow if only a 100 per cent increase in capacity is met within 12 months? Or a 25 per cent increase?

- Environmental Vision, goals, strategies and tactics fundamental to the ethos of the business – could they cause conflict with the strategic initiative?

## SECTION 2: DETAILED FINDINGS

*Joe, Director of Supply Chain and Customer Relations, Strategic Initiative Lead*

Interviewed 10 March 2015 by Karl Cox and A.N. Other

*Quotes:*

> *'We've been stuck in the same market, same product, same suppliers, in a rut, for about five years now. There are few competitors but they've*

*always been there. This last year, we've lost out on a couple of large orders because our potato suppliers have been smaller farms.'*

*'We have got to find a way to meet the new massive demand for potatoes.'*

*'We need a monitoring system in place to tell us the crop and potato availability to handle large orders.'*

*Key points:*

- initiative vision: to increase potato supply to meet and exceed the projected demand over the next five years;

- be ready to supply the EU market;

- deliver on customer orders faster than previously;

- improve potato process: centralise storage and use IT to monitor crop readiness;

- increase capacity by 200 per cent within 12 months;

- reduce potato quality assessment by two days;

- adhere to our Environmental Vision and Strategies: ethical farming practices, no chemicals, pesticides or GMO.

There appears to be a gap in planning between the 12-month capacity increase and the five-year Vision. It is not clear how the 12-month capacity increase will be achieved, or what happens if that target is not met.

[Add more interview material here and so on]

## Strategic Goal Model: Potato Grow strategic initiative

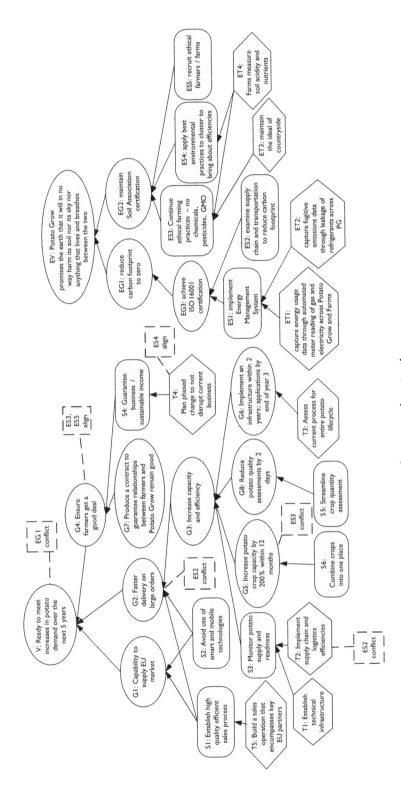

Figure 6.1    Strategic initiative Potato Grow: goals, strategies, tactics

Figure 6.1 represents a view of the strategic initiative for Potato Grow. The model is derived and developed from the interview findings and supported by the data.

As can be seen, there are four main, interwoven threads to achieving the Vision:

1.   capability to handle large and EU orders (Goal 1);

2.   ensure faster delivery on orders (Goal 2);

3.   achieve targeted capacity increase (Goal 3);

4.   ensure the farmer gets a good deal and remains loyal (Goal 4).

There is also an Environmental Strategy in place, with a bold Vision of not harming the earth in any way, with supporting key Environmental Goals:

1.   reduce carbon footprint to zero (Environmental Goal 1);

2.   maintain Soil Association certification (Environmental Goal 2);

3.   continue ethical farming practices – no chemicals, pesticides, GMO (Environmental Strategy 3).

It is clear that not everything is aligned and indeed the Environmental Strategy is in conflict with the business strategy, not least the Business Vision in conflict with the Environmental Goal 1: Reduce carbon footprint to zero. However, most of the models are well aligned.

Figure 6.2 shows the strategic context for the Potato Grow initiative and what partner is responsible for what goals, strategies and tactics.

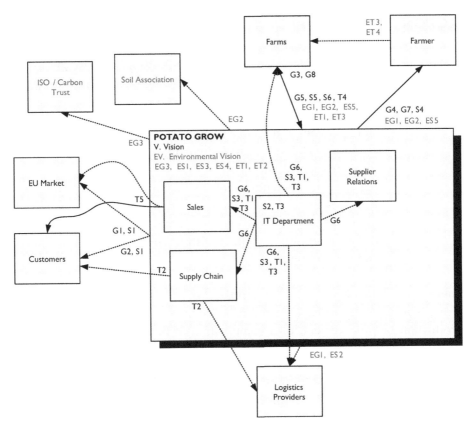

**Figure 6.2    Potato Grow strategic context**

- Potato Grow is responsible for delivering on its Vision across all the departments.

- As a whole, Potato Grow is responsible for achieving Goal 1: Capability to Supply the EU market, obviously specifically targeted at the EU market partner.

- The supply chain department within Potato Grow is responsible for implementing supply chain and logistics efficiencies (Tactic 2) in conjunction with Potato Grow's logistics providers.

[and so on ... to give as complete description of the model as you think necessary. There's no need to explain every single point, just give an example or two of each to explain how the model is read and the key message it conveys.]

## SECTION 3: CONFLICTS AND OPPORTUNITIES

1.    Goal 5: Increase Potato Crop capacity by 200 per cent within 12 months is a challenge. The underlying physical and software infrastructures are not in place to:

   - store potatoes in the same place;
   - monitor stock levels against demand;
   - measure capacity increase;
   - register the potential environmental impact of dramatic increases in crop size: damage done to the soil, depletion of the water table, energy consumption increase creating a larger carbon footprint, in conflict with Environmental Goals 1 and 2 and supporting strategies.

There is also little idea about what happens beyond 12 months and up to five years. Is it necessary to have such a massive increase in capacity and hence production or procurement, or a combination of both in such a short time frame? What are the alternative scenarios?

There is an opportunity for Potato Grow to consider the usage of more renewable energy sources, more environmental friendly farming methods and products and to set the sustainability and environmental agenda for the industry.

[and so on ... you would add more detail to the opportunities but don't over-do the detail. It's an opportunity to give your client an idea of what to do but not how; the how is you next contract.]

## APPENDICES

The following appendices present supporting materials and data.

Appendix A:

   •   Potato Grow Business strategy table (Table 6.1)

   •   Potato Grow environmental strategy table (Table 6.2)

Table 6.1   Potato Grow business strategy

| Business Strategy | Main Partner | Supporting Partners | Helps Achieve |
|---|---|---|---|
| **VISION** | | | |
| V: Ready to meet increases in potato demand over the next five years. | Potato Grow | — | — |
| **Goals** | | | |
| G1: Capability to supply EU market. | Potato Grow | EU market | V |
| G2: Faster delivery on large orders. | Potato Grow | Customers | V |
| G3: Increase capacity and efficiency of farms. | Farms | Potato Grow | G1, G2 |
| G4: Ensure farmers get a good deal. | Potato Grow | Farmer | V |
| G5: Increase potato crop capacity by 200 per cent within 12 months. | Potato Grow | Farms | G3 |
| G6: Implement an infrastructure within two years; applications by end of year 3. | IT dept | Potato Grow, farms, logistics, supply chain, sales, supplier relations | G3 |
| G7: Produce a contract to guarantee relationships between farmers and Potato Grow remain good. | Potato Grow | Farmers | G4 |
| G8: Reduce potato quality assessments by two days. | Farms | Potato Grow | G3 |
| **Strategies** | | | |
| S1: Establish high-quality efficient sales process. | Sales | Customers, EU market | G1, G2 |
| S2: Avoid use of smart and mobile technologies. | IT dept | Potato Grow | G1, G2 |
| S3: Monitor potato supply and readiness. | IT dept | Farms, sales, logistic providers | G3 |
| S4: Guarantee business/sustainable income. | Potato Grow | Farmer | G4 |
| S5: Streamline crop quantity assessment. | Potato Grow | Farms | G8 |
| S6: Combine crops in one place. | Potato Grow | Farms | G5 |
| **Tactics** | | | |
| T1: Establish technical infrastructure. | IT dept | Farms, sales, logistic providers | S3 |
| T2: Implement supply chain and logistics efficiencies. | Supply Chain | Logistics providers, customers | S3 |
| T3: Assess current process for entire potato lifecycle. | IT dept | Potato Grow, farms, logistics, supply chain, sales, supplier relations | G6 |
| T4: Plan phased change to not disrupt current business. | Potato Grow | Farms | S4 |
| T5: Build a sales operation that encompasses key EU partners. | Sales | EU market, customers | S1 |

**Table 6.2** Potato Grow environmental strategy

| Business Strategy | Owner/Involves | Impacts/Conflicts with | Supports/Aligns to |
|---|---|---|---|
| **VISION** | | | |
| EV: Potato Grow promises the earth that it will in no way harm its soil nor its sky nor anything that lives and breathes between the two. | Potato Grow | Everything | Everything |
| **Goals** | | | |
| EG1: Reduce carbon footprint to zero. | Potato Grow | Farms, farmers, logistics providers, *Initiative Vision* | EVision |
| EG2: Maintain Soil Association certification. | Potato Grow/Soil Association | Farms, farmers | EVision |
| EG3: Achieve ISO16001 certification. | Potato Grow/ISO, Carbon Trust | Potato Grow | EG1 |
| **Strategies** | | | |
| ES1: Implement Energy Management System. | Potato Grow | Potato Grow | EG3 |
| ES2: Examine supply chain and transportation to reduce carbon footprint. | Potato Grow | Logistics providers, *Initiative G2, T2* | EG3 |
| ES3: Continue ethical farming practices – no chemicals, pesticides and GMOs. | Potato Grow, farms, farmers | *Initiative G5* | *Initiative G4*, EG2 |
| ES4: Apply best environmental practices to cluster to bring about efficiencies. | Potato Grow, farms, farmers | — | *Initiative T4*, EG2 |
| ES5: Recruit ethical farmers/ farms. | Potato Grow | Farms, farmers | *Initiative G4*, EG2 |
| **Tactics** | | | |
| ET1: Capture emissions data through automated meter reading of gas and electricity across Potato Grow and farms. | Potato Grow | Potato Grow, farms | ES1 |
| ET2: Capture fugitive emissions data through leakage of refrigerants across Potato Grow. | Potato Grow | Potato Grow | ES1 |
| ET3: Measure soil acidity and nutrients. | Potato Grow, Farmers | Farms | ES3 |
| ET4: Maintain the ideal of countryside. | Farmers | Farms | ES3, ES4 |

## Making the Executive Pitch: Slides and Speech

You will have noticed the trend in the reports described above. The one-pager is a microcosm of the interim report which itself is a microcosm of the full report. You are building one structure only. The benefits are that your client will be 'used' to seeing the same format and so will not have to learn the document layout again and again.

The same goes for slideware. Keep to a similar format. You're obviously constrained by visibility when it comes to slides. There's only so much you can squeeze onto a slide and have it considered not only readable but understood, short, sharp and strong.

There are many excellent publications on how to present[2] so I'm not going to talk too much about this other than give a few pointers that have been valuable for me when making these presentations.

### WHAT TO KEEP OUT OF THE SLIDES AND WHAT TO LEAVE IN

It's an odd way to look at it but the hardest part about the presentation is knowing what *not* to talk about. Normally the 'what not to talk about' consists of the massive detail you have picked up during the engagement. Remember your audience are executives: they want the high-level view but they also have to be convinced you know why the high-level view is as it is.

*Do* put the key points into each slide only. Be careful about minute detail of each point. No one will want to read the minutiae, nor will anyone want to listen to you drone on about a tiny point for minutes at end. If you do talk about details then you really need to be picky about which one or two (at most) points you want to elaborate upon. There has to be a good reason for you to do so; showing how knowledgeable you are is not one of them.

Be wary about using names. Never, ever mention names – I've said this before but it's important to repeat. If you're asked: 'Who said that?' state that all comments were confidentially gathered as agreed with your client. If you do give a name because you've got prior agreement from your client and the individual interviewee to do so, ensure the comment is very positive *and* enlightening.

---

2   For example, take a look at: David Booth, Deborah Shames and Peter Desberg *Own the Room: Business Presentations that Persuade, Engage, and Get Results*, New York, McGraw-Hill Professional 2009.

An enlightening comment is one that sheds new light or a new take on some information. Make sure your client has already bought into the comment and has agreed to back you up if needed, prior to the presentation. Don't give names to negative comments – and avoid specific job titles too.

Models such as the business strategy models seen in this chapter are hard to read in slides. Given the complexity of realistic business strategy and partner models, showing these in a slide presentation will only cause problems: (1) you'll spend a long time explaining the notation; (2) you'll get a barrage of comments of which a large percentage will be negative or 'that's not right' comment.

Other models or figures such as bar charts or magic quadrants are well known and are much easier to interpret and explain, so keep those in, if you have them and they are useful. Remember, though, that they are not strategy models and serve a completely different purpose. If you do present a strategy model then do so only when your client insists you do so.

Tables are good. A good table is very expressive and covers a lot of ground very quickly. Tables are easy to read provided they are in a simple format. Keep the wording in tables short because there is a high risk of clutter that you resolve by making the font too small to read. Tables should be uncluttered and sentences short; font should be a good size to be read easily and comfortably from the back of the room.

Each slide should have only about three bullet points; psychologists recognise that with three, people can recall about 90 per cent content. Beyond three, this level of recall drops dramatically. Each bullet should be a single sentence. The spoken word matters as much as your slide; if your slide words do not match your spoken word then your audience will be confused. Read the slide point and then elaborate for a few minutes.

Keep the slides fairly plain: white background, dark text or dark background and white text: you never see movie subtitles written in black as the background colours will change continually. Slides are different in that one respect. Be consistent – don't chop and change layout through a presentation. Make sure colour blind people can see the colours and contrasts. I'm colour blind so I know this matters: pastels just don't wash. And use your company's template, assuming it is any good.

Be convincing when you speak and in how you move. You've got to convince people that you know what you're talking about, that you are an authority on the matter at hand. You do this with evidence and expression of knowledge, not with a big stick. Make sure you know your context and the details of the engagement findings. You will have to back up your points with detail as well as answer searching questions from your audience. You have to believe in what you are presenting: what you state matters as much to you as it does to your audience.

The slides have to be credible to your client. The client should see your slides before they are presented to her peers and management. Your client will normally censor and remove what is unacceptable, unswallowable, undefendable and irrelevant. Hopefully the vast majority of your slides will remain unaffected. I would not be tempted to remove any controversial points until you have shown your client. You never know what she might let you get away with. Also, the more controversial points that remain, the more likely your client's company is willing to take on the findings, and the more likely you will get more work. If your audience begins to argue strongly against your findings, it may be they not ready to change. If your client asks you to deliberately hide anything or change anything they view as a risk they could do without, politely refuse.

Your client will pick up on the inevitable spelling mistakes, which is a good thing and may suggest additions: what did you miss, what is the hot topic now and is it addressed here?

I want to reiterate this point: Don't read from card prompts. Practice your presentation, practice again and then again and in front of colleagues. Reading from cards gives the newsreader impression: just passing on someone else's findings and not your own. It's strange that I've seen cards used primarily by defence industry presenters who stand rigid with hands glued to the podium whilst giving a monotone and uninspiring talk. No one walks away convinced by that kind of presentation. Keep still but not static. You've got to move but not frenetically. Don't bound around the room like a gazelle, don't hop from side to side with nervous energy. Equally don't become a statue and freeze in the one position. Relax and breathe!

Move occasionally from one side of the screen to the next – dependent upon where your slide changer is and where everyone is sitting in the room. Look at your audience's line of sight and work out the best place to be in order to minimise blocking the slides but maximise your presence. Smile, be positive and people will believe you. Look your audience in the eye. Making eye contact shows them you are convinced of your findings and goes 80 per cent of the way to convincing them.

Finally, tell the truth.

One last key point is time. Keep to the agreed presentation time. If you've only got 15 minutes and 10 key points, spread the time equally between the points. Don't rush or slow down on some points and neglect the others. You will have to practice to be able to do this well. I was once at a conference somewhere in Europe where a presenter had far too many slides and was told he was running out of time. Instead of doing the sensible thing and summarising or highlighting the key point per remaining slide, he simply talked faster on every single point on every single slide, so fast in fact that most of the audience, including me, couldn't follow any of it. This is not a good way to present. So practice some more. Initially, follow a timing rule of thumb: aim for about five minutes per slide.

If you've only got 15 minutes to present then you really only want three to four slides. That means focus is key and all points should be short, sharp and strong. There's room for manoeuvre but the best rule is to keep it simple.

## Presenting to the Masses

It's often the case you'll need to present to a lot of staff at the same time, a mass audience such as the entire IT department or the customer relations division. Normally you'll get more time to do this than in presenting to executives, though the way you present is going to be exactly the same. If there are any differences, these could be:

- the time to present will be longer (probably, but not by much);

- there will be a more operational focus, to make the presentation more relevant to your audience;

- the opportunity to provide more detail is greater, but remember to keep an eye on the clock;

- you are more likely to get derisory comments – take these as compliments because you are probably finding the sore spots! Ask why the audience member is being critical. What did you get wrong about the point? If you got it wrong, say thank you for the correction.

I suggest you follow the guidance presented in 'Making the Executive Pitch'. The slides should look the same. You might add more detail when presenting to a larger audience but these will be on separate slides, not all crammed on the same one.

Again, the golden rule is to practice, practice and practice. Get your client to agree on the slides. Also run the slides by the departmental/divisional managers for approval prior to dissemination if you've been asked to do so and do it anyway if you haven't. You want to get management buy-in prior to presenting to the masses.

## Summary

This chapter has discussed presentation styles and formats: what to put into a document and slides and how to present the results. I always go by the rule of short, sharp and strong. The examples presented here are for your use if you think the structure of document makes sense to you. As ever, use what is useful but be mindful of what you discard. I'm not keen on templates per se because they remove the need to think and replace cranial capacity with box ticking and gap filling. As I have repeatedly said, context dictates what you do. Make sure your presentation fits the context of your client's environment.

# Concluding Remarks

This book has taken you through a constructive journey of planning and running interviews, then conducting analysis, deriving and building strategic models and presenting results back. The opportunity before you now is to take the ideas from this book you think worthwhile and to apply them successfully to your advantage.

If I were to take the key rungs of opportunity away from this book, they would, in no particular order, be:

1.  Learn your context – take the time to understand your client's business and the specifics of the project you are being hired for. That way, you'll be considered an equal rather than an uninformed outsider.

2.  Plan what you intend to do – otherwise you'll make the silly mistakes I made; the planning checklist in Chapter 1 is really useful for this.

3.  Plan specific questions in advance – if it doesn't matter what you ask about, it doesn't matter what you find out.

4.  Be flexible – if you find your initial questions are off the mark, change them but double check to make sure you're back on track.

5.  Be ruthless – if you're going off course in an interview, pull it back in line as fast as you can. Time is money and you can't afford to squander either.

6.  Two heads are better than one – have two people conduct the interview. That way you won't have to watch, write, talk and listen all at the same time. If your recording device fails, your partner can fix it or write more notes while you speak, not slowing you down and, importantly, not delaying your interviewee.

7.    Make sure you understand your model before trying to convince a client.

8.    Always be brave in your assertions but not foolhardy.

9.    Be grateful for the support and feedback of your client when they do not understand the model – it is a help to you to clarify again what you are doing.

10.   If you are getting lost in the modelling just forget it because if you are lost your client will have no idea at all.

11.   If time is really short, just model the context rather than the goals but include the goal references in the context.

12.   Putting the context with the goal is very powerful.

13.   Don't forget it takes time to model so model only that which needs or demands it.

14.   Be nice to your model – make it clear, readable and easy to adapt.

15.   Accept that you know far less about your client's business than they do and accept when you have missed what is obvious to them.

16.   Present your findings, recommendations and results in a similar format – it saves on work and keeps things consistent; accuracy is your own look out!

17.   Keep your message short, sharp and strong. Add detail only when absolutely imperative to do so.

18.   Be polite, positive, punctual, proactive and professional – your job is to solve problems so solve them with a smile, with erudition and wisdom ... and do it on time. If you see problems or issues that could affect the successful conclusion of the project, fix them if you can. If you can't, get your client to fix them.

19.   Hypnotise – you've got to be so convincing that people believe you, as if your findings are second nature to them, and matter deeply. More often than not, companies want someone to tell them what

they already know but are culturally too paralysed to act upon. You are the enabler. You've got to break down the walls company cultures and individuals always build up, in order to bring about change for the greater good of your client, and for the world.

Follow the steps in planning where appropriate, and run your interviews in an organised, repeatable manner, then your analysis and results presentations will go smoother and your kudos will grow.

## Summary

This book has taken you on a journey into the not so obvious world of planning and running interviews. Chapters 1 and 2 explored how to go about planning in general and then specifically for an interview. Chapter 3 then examined an interview in depth, identifying key elements such as strategy, goals and context. This in and of itself is useful but analysis is required to work out what the key points are that your clients need to be discovered and expressed to ensure their strategic requirements are correct. Chapter 4 showed how to conduct quick content analysis and then how to tabulate the results accordingly. A picture paints more than a thousand words. Chapter 5 explains and shows you how to simply create complex and highly expressive goal and context models as a means of validating visually those strategic requirements. Visualisation is a powerful tool. But this is still not the full story because your client would like to see a coherent report and presentation. These are detailed in Chapter 6 using the example case study.

# Index

For Product Safety Concerns and Information please contact our EU
representative GPSR@taylorandfrancis.com Taylor & Francis Verlag GmbH,
Kaufingerstraße 24, 80331 München, Germany

Printed and bound by CPI Group (UK) Ltd, Croydon, CR0 4YY
01/05/2025
01858393-0001